Learning Kibana 5.0

Exploit the visualization capabilities of Kibana and build powerful interactive dashboards

Bahaaldine Azarmi

BIRMINGHAM - MUMBAI

Learning Kibana 5.0

First published: February 2017

Production reference: 1100217

Published by Packt Publishing Ltd.
Livery Place
35 Livery Street
Birmingham
B3 2PB, UK.
ISBN 978-1-78646-300-5

www.packtpub.com

Credits

Author

Bahaaldine Azarmi

Reviewers

Alan Hardy
Bharvi Dixit

Commissioning Editor

Amey Varangaonkar

Acquisition Editor

Prachi Bisht

Content Development Editor

Manthan Raja

Technical Editor

Dharmendra Yadav

Copy Editor

Safis Editing

Project Coordinator

Nidhi Joshi

Proofreader

Safis Editing

Indexer

Aishwarya Gangawane

Graphics

Tania Dutta

Production Coordinator

Nilesh Mohite

About the Author

Bahaaldine Azarmi, Baha for short, is a Solutions Architect at Elastic. Prior to this position, Baha co-founded reachfive, a marketing data-platform focused on user behavior and social analytics. Baha also worked for different software vendors such as, Talend or Oracle, where he held the positions of Solutions Architect and Architect. Before *Learning Kibana 5.0*, Baha authored books such as *Scalable Big Data Architecture*, by *Apress* and *Talend for Big Data*, by *Packt Publishing*. Baha is based in Paris and has a Master's Degree in computer science from Polytech'Paris.

There are a few people I would like to acknowledge, as this book is not just me writing chapters but the work of many folks from Elastic regrouped into one book:

- Alan Hardy, EMEA Director of Solutions Architecture, for his mentoring, support, and for his excellent review
- Steve Mayzak, VP of Solutions Architecture, for supporting innovation in the SA team and me writing this book :-)
- Christian Dahlqvist, Solution Architect, for providing the Apache web logs demo used in Chapter 4, *Logging Analytics with Kibana 5.0*
- Rich Collier, Steve Dodson, and Sophie Chang, respectively Solutions Architect, Machine Learning Tech, and Team Lead, for helping me to understand the concept of anomaly detection and providing the demo used in Chapter 8, *Anomaly Detection in Kibana 5.0*
- Court Ewing and Spencer Alger, respectively Tech Lead and Javascript Developer, and actually, the whole Kibana team, for answering all my questions!

About the Reviewers

Alan Hardy has spent over 20 years in the software industry with a breadth of experience in different businesses and environments, from multinationals to software startups and financial organizations, including global trading and exchanges. He started out as a developer on real-time, monitoring, and alerting systems before moving into packet-switching technology and financial data processing in C, C++, and Java-based environments. Alan now works for Elastic, where he gets to fully explore his data-wrangling passion, leading EMEA Solution Architecture.

Bharvi Dixit is an IT professional and an engineer with extensive experience of working on the search servers, NoSQL databases and cloud services. He holds a master's degree in computer science and is currently working with Sentieo, a USA-based financial data and equity research platform where he leads the overall platform and architecture of the company, spanning hundreds of servers. At Sentieo, he also plays a key role in the search and data team.

He is also the organizer of Delhi's Elasticsearch Meetup Group, where he speaks about Elasticsearch and Lucene and continuously building the community around these technologies.

Bharvi also works as a freelance Elasticsearch consultant and has helped more than half a dozen organizations adapt Elasticsearch to solve their complex search problems in different use cases, such as creating search solutions for big data-automated intelligence platforms in the area of counter-terrorism and risk management, as well as in other domains, such as recruitment, e-commerce, finance, social search, and log monitoring.

He has a keen interest in creating scalable backend platforms. His other areas of interest are search engineering, data analytics, and distributed computing. Java and Python are the primary languages in which he loves to write code, and he has also built proprietary software for consultancy firms.

In 2013, he started working on Lucene and Elasticsearch, and has authored two books on Elasticsearch, *Elasticsearch Essentials* and *Mastering Elasticsearch 5.0*, both published by *Packt Publishing*.

You can connect with him on LinkedIn at `https://in.linkedin.com/in/bharvidixit` or can be followed on Twitter `@d_bharvi`.

www.PacktPub.com

For support files and downloads related to your book, please visit www.PacktPub.com.

Did you know that Packt offers eBook versions of every book published, with PDF and ePub files available? You can upgrade to the eBook version at www.PacktPub.com and as a print book customer, you are entitled to a discount on the eBook copy. Get in touch with us at service@packtpub.com for more details.

At www.PacktPub.com, you can also read a collection of free technical articles, sign up for a range of free newsletters and receive exclusive discounts and offers on Packt books and eBooks.

https://www.packtpub.com/mapt

Get the most in-demand software skills with Mapt. Mapt gives you full access to all Packt books and video courses, as well as industry-leading tools to help you plan your personal development and advance your career.

Why subscribe?

- Fully searchable across every book published by Packt
- Copy and paste, print, and bookmark content
- On demand and accessible via a web browser

Customer Feedback

Thanks for purchasing this Packt book. At Packt, quality is at the heart of our editorial process. To help us improve, please leave us an honest review on this book's Amazon page at `https://www.amazon.com/Learning-Kibana-5-0-Bahaaldine-Azarmi-ebook/dp/B01L Z4ESK0/`.

If you'd like to join our team of regular reviewers, you can email us at `customerreviews@packtpub.com`. We award our regular reviewers with free eBooks and videos in exchange for their valuable feedback. Help us be relentless in improving our products!

For Aurelia, June, and Colin-Harper

Table of Contents

Preface

Today, understanding data, whatever the nature of the data is, keeps getting harder. They are couple of reasons for that such as the volume, the variety of data, the pace at which the data is created and the complexity to correlate data from different sources.

It's hard for anyone to cope with this constant increasing challenge, that's why more and more applications are built to facilitate data management, at every level: ingesting data, processing data, storing data, and ultimately visualizing the data to understand it.

All those levels put together are the fundamental layers to build a data-driven architecture that needs to scale with a growing demand and expectation from users.

There is tons of software and applications out there that could answer those challenges, but rarely will you find a stack that could fulfill all the requirements altogether and across many types of use cases.

The Elastic Stack is one of them: it gives the user a way to access their data in an agile and scalable way. Kibana is part of the Elastic Stack and provide a visualization layer on top of data indexed in Elasticsearch, the storage layer.

In *Learning Kibana 5.0*, we'll go through the holistic visualization experience that Kibana offers to address very different use cases, such as creating dashboards using accidents data, or building statistics on top system data, or even detecting anomalies in data.

Rather than listing and going through Kibana features one by one, this book adopts a pragmatic approach where you will learn based on concrete examples and hands-on.

What this book covers

Chapter 1, *Introduction to Data-Driven Architecture*, describes the fundamental layers that compose a data-driven architecture, and how the Elastic Stack can be used to build it.

Chapter 2, *Installing and Setting up Kibana 5.0*, covers the installation of Elasticsearch and Kibana, and a walkthrough in Kibana 5.0 anatomy.

Chapter 3, *Business Analytics with Kibana 5.0*, tackles the first use case of this book, namely business analytics, with the help of Paris accidentology data.

Chapter 4, *Logging Analytics with Kibana 5.0,* covers a technical logging use case on top of Apache logs data.

Chapter 5, *Metric Analytics with Metricbeat and Kibana 5.0,* walks the reader through the brand new feature of metrics analytics in Kibana 5.0 with the help of system data from Metricbeat.

Chapter 6, *Graph Exploration in Kibana,* explains the concept of graphs in the Elastic Stack and introduces forensic graph analysis on top of Stack Overflow data.

Chapter 7, *Customizing Kibana 5.0 Timelion,* shows how to extend the capabilities of Timelion and build an extension to fetch data from Google Analytics.

Chapter 8, *Anomaly Detection in Kibana 5.0,* covers the Elastic Stack machine learning features and how to use Kibana to visualize anomalies on top of system data.

Chapter 9, *Creating a Custom Plugin for Kibana 5.0,* explains how to create a plugin to visualize the Elasticsearch cluster topology.

What you need for this book

In this book, you will need to download and install the Elastic Stack, specifically, Elasticsearch, Kibana, Metricbeat, Logstash, and the X-Pack. All the software is available from the following page: http://www.elastic.co/downloads.

The Elastic Stack can be run on a various environment on commodity machines; here is the support matrix: https://www.elastic.co/support/matrix.

Who this book is for

This book is for developers, operation teams, business analytics, and data architects who want to learn how to deploy a data-driven architecture using the Elastic Stack 5.0, and more specifically, how to enable visualization on top of the data indexed in Elasticsearch with Kibana 5.0.

Conventions

In this book, you will find a number of text styles that distinguish between different kinds of information. Here are some examples of these styles and an explanation of their meaning.

Code words in text, database table names, folder names, filenames, file extensions, pathnames, dummy URLs, user input, and Twitter handles are shown as follows: "We can include other contexts through the use of the include directive."

A block of code is set as follows:

```
PUT /_snapshot/basic_logstash_repository
{
  "type": "fs",
  "settings": {
  "location":
    "/Users/bahaaldine/Dropbox/Packt/sources/chapter3/
      basic_logstash_repository",
  "compress": true
  }
}
```

Any command-line input or output is written as follows:

```
GET _cat/indices/basic*
```

New terms and **important words** are shown in bold. Words that you see on the screen, for example, in menus or dialog boxes, appear in the text like this: "Clicking the **Next** button moves you to the next screen."

Warnings or important notes appear in a box like this.

Tips and tricks appear like this.

Reader feedback

Feedback from our readers is always welcome. Let us know what you think about this book—what you liked or disliked. Reader feedback is important for us as it helps us develop titles that you will really get the most out of.

To send us general feedback, simply e-mail feedback@packtpub.com, and mention the book's title in the subject of your message.

If there is a topic that you have expertise in and you are interested in either writing or contributing to a book, see our author guide at www.packtpub.com/authors.

Customer support

Now that you are the proud owner of a Packt book, we have a number of things to help you to get the most from your purchase.

Downloading the example code

You can download the example code files for this book from your account at http://www.packtpub.com. If you purchased this book elsewhere, you can visit http://www.packtpub.com/support and register to have the files e-mailed directly to you.

You can download the code files by following these steps:

1. Log in or register to our website using your e-mail address and password.
2. Hover the mouse pointer on the **SUPPORT** tab at the top.
3. Click on **Code Downloads & Errata**.
4. Enter the name of the book in the **Search** box.
5. Select the book for which you're looking to download the code files.
6. Choose from the drop-down menu where you purchased this book from.
7. Click on **Code Download**.

You can also download the code files by clicking on the **Code Files** button on the book's webpage at the Packt Publishing website. This page can be accessed by entering the book's name in the **Search** box. Please note that you need to be logged in to your Packt account.

Once the file is downloaded, please make sure that you unzip or extract the folder using the latest version of:

- WinRAR / 7-Zip for Windows
- Zipeg / iZip / UnRarX for Mac
- 7-Zip / PeaZip for Linux

The code bundle for the book is also hosted on GitHub at https://github.com/PacktPublishing/Learning-Kibana-5. We also have other code bundles from our rich catalog of books and videos available at https://github.com/PacktPublishing/. Check them out!

Downloading the color images of this book

We also provide you with a PDF file that has color images of the screenshots/diagrams used in this book. The color images will help you better understand the changes in the output. You can download this file from `https://www.packtpub.com/sites/default/files/down loads/LearningKibana5_ColorImages.pdf`.

Errata

Although we have taken every care to ensure the accuracy of our content, mistakes do happen. If you find a mistake in one of our books—maybe a mistake in the text or the code—we would be grateful if you could report this to us. By doing so, you can save other readers from frustration and help us improve subsequent versions of this book. If you find any errata, please report them by visiting `http://www.packtpub.com/submit-errata`, selecting your book, clicking on the **Errata Submission Form** link, and entering the details of your errata. Once your errata are verified, your submission will be accepted and the errata will be uploaded to our website or added to any list of existing errata under the **Errata** section of that title.

To view the previously submitted errata, go to `https://www.packtpub.com/books/conten t/support` and enter the name of the book in the search field. The required information will appear under the **Errata** section.

Piracy

Piracy of copyrighted material on the Internet is an ongoing problem across all media. At Packt, we take the protection of our copyright and licenses very seriously. If you come across any illegal copies of our works in any form on the Internet, please provide us with the location address or website name immediately so that we can pursue a remedy.

Please contact us at `copyright@packtpub.com` with a link to the suspected pirated material.

We appreciate your help in protecting our authors and our ability to bring you valuable content.

Questions

If you have a problem with any aspect of this book, you can contact us at `questions@packtpub.com`, and we will do our best to address the problem.

1
Introduction to Data-Driven Architecture

If you are reading this book, it certainly means that you and I have something in common: we are both looking for a solution to effectively visualize and understand our data.

Data can be anything: business data, infrastructure data, accounting data, numbers, strings, structured, or unstructured. In any case, all organizations reach a point where trying to understand data and extract the value of it begins to be a real challenge, for different reasons:

- **Data brings complexity**: If we take the example of an e-commerce IT operation team where one must find why the orders just dropped, it can be a very tricky process to go to the log to get the issue.
- **Data comes from a variety of sources**: Infrastructure, applications, devices, legacy systems, databases, and so on. Most of the time, you need to correlate them. In the e-commerce example, maybe the drop is due to an issue in my database?
- **Data increases at a very fast pace**: Data growth implies some new questions, such as which data should I keep? Or how do I scale my data management infrastructure?

The good news is that you won't need to learn it the hard way, as I'll try in this book to explain how I've tackled data analytics projects for different use cases and for different types of data based on my experience.

The other good news is that I'm part of the **Solutions Architecture** (**SA**) team at Elastic, and guess what? We'll use the Elastic stack. By being part of the SA team, I'm involved in a variety of use cases, from small to large scale, with different industries; the main goal is always to give to our users better management of and access to their data, and a better way to understand their data.

In this book, we'll dig into the use of Kibana, the data analytics layer of the Elastic stack. Kibana is the data visualization layer used in an overall data-driven architecture.

But what is data-driven architecture? This is the concept I will illustrate in this chapter by going through industry challenges, the usual technology used to answer this need, and then we'll go into the description of the Elastic stack.

Industry challenges

Depending on the industry, the use cases can be very different in term of data usage. Within a given industry, data is used in different ways for different purposes, whether it's for security analytics or order management.

Data comes in various formats and different scales of volumes. In the telecommunications industry, it's very common to see a project about the quality of services where data is grabbed from 100,000 network devices.

In every case, it always comes down to the same canonical issues:

* How to decrease the complexity of handling fast growing data at scale
* How to enable my organization to visualize data in the most effective and real-time fashion

By solving these fundamental issues, organizations would be allowed to simply recognize visual patterns without having to deal with the burden of exploring tons of data

To help you get a better understanding of the actual challenges, we'll start by describing the common use cases met across industries and then see what technologies are used and their limits in addressing these challenges.

Use cases

Every application produces data, whether it be in daily life when you use your favorite map application to geo-locate yourself and the best restaurant around you; or be it in IT organizations, with the different technical layers involved in building recommendations depending on your location and profile.

All computers and the processes and applications running on them are continuously producing data, effectively capturing the state of the system "now", driven by a CPU tick or user click.

This data normally stays in obscure files, located physically on the computer and hidden deep within data centers. We need a means to extract this data (ship), convert it from obscure data formats (transform), and eventually store it for centralized access.

This flow of data streaming in the system, based on event triggering functional processes, needs a proper architecture to be shipped, transformed, stored, and accessed in a scalable and distributed way.

The way we interact with applications dramatically changed the legacy architecture paradigm that we used to lay out. It's not anymore about building relational databases, it's about spin up on demand distributed data stores based on the throughput; it's not only about having batch processing data overnight, but it's also about pushing data processing to boundaries that weren't met so far in terms of real-time and machine learning aspects; it's not anymore about relying on heavy business intelligence tools to build reporting, but more about an iterative approach to data visualization close to real-time insights.

End users, driven by the need to process increasingly higher volumes of data, while maintaining real-time query responses, have turned away from more traditional, relational database or data warehousing solutions, due to poor scalability or performance. The solution is increasingly found in highly distributed, clustered data stores that can easily be.

Take the example of application monitoring, which is one of the most common use cases we meet across industries. Each application logs data, sometimes in a centralized way, for example by using syslog, and sometimes all the logs are spread out across the infrastructure, which makes it hard to have a single point of access to the data stream.

When an issue happens, or simply when you need to access the data, you might need to get:

- **The location**: where the logs are stored.
- **The permission**: can I access the logs? If not, who should I contact to get them?
- **The understanding of the log structure**: I can take here the example of Tuxedo with multiline logs, which is not a trivial task at all.

The majority of large organizations don't retain logged data for longer than the duration of a log file rotation (a few hours or even minutes). This means that by the time an issue has occurred, the data which could provide the answers is lost.

When you actually have the data, what do you do? Well, there are different ways to extract the gist of logs. A lot of people start by using a simple string pattern search (GREP). Essentially, they try to find matching patterns in logs using a regular expression. That might work for a single log file but that doesn't scale as the log files rotate and you want to get insights over time, plus the fact that you may have more than one application and the need to make correlations.

Without any context regarding an issue (no time range, no application key, no insight), a user is reduced to brute force, assuming you are also looking in the correct file in the first place.

GREP is convenient, but clearly doesn't fit the need to react quickly to failure in order to reduce the **Mean Time To Recovery (MTTR)**. Think about it: what if we are talking of a major issue on the purchase API of an e-commerce website? What if the users experience a high latency on this page or, worse, can't go to the end of the purchase process? The time you will spend trying to recover your application from gigabytes of logs is money you could potentially lose.

Another potential issue could be around a lack of security analytics and not being able to blacklist the IPs that try to brute force your application. In the same context, I've seen use cases where people didn't know that every night there was a group of IPs attempting to get into their system, and this was just because they were not able to visualize the IPs on a map and trigger alerts based on their value.

A simple, yet very effective, pattern in order to protect a system would have been to limit access to resources or services to the internal system only. The ability to whitelist access to a known set of IP addresses is essential.

The consequence could be dramatic if a proper data-driven architecture with a solid visualization layer is not serving those needs: lack of visibility and control, increasing the MTTR, customer dissatisfaction, financial impact, security leaks, and bad response time and user experience.

Fundamental steps

The objective is then to avoid these consequences, and build an architecture that will serve the different following aspects.

Data shipping

The architecture should be able to transport any kind of data/events, structured or unstructured; in other words, move data from remote machines to a centralized location. This is usually done by a lightweight agent deployed next to the data sources, on the same host, or on a distant host with regards to different aspects:

- Lightweight, because ideally it shouldn't compete for resources with the process that generates the actual data, otherwise it could reduce the expected process performance
- There are a lot of data shipping technologies out there; some of them are tight to a specific technology, others are based on an extensible framework which can adapt relatively to a data source
- Shipping data is not only about sending data over the wire, it's also about security and being sure that the data is sent to the proper destination with an end-to-end secured pipeline.
- Another aspect of data shipping is the management of data load. Shipping data should be done relative to the load that the end destination is able to ingest; this feature is called back pressure management

It's essential for data visualization to rely on reliable data shipping. Take as an example data flowing from financial trade machines and how critical it could be not to be able to detect a security leak just because you are losing data.

Data ingest

The scope of an ingest layer is to receive data, encompassing as wide a range of commonly used transport protocols and data formats as possible, while providing capabilities to extract and transform this data before finally storing it.

Processing data can somehow be seen as **extracting, transforming, and loading** (ETL) data, which is often called an ingestion pipeline and essentially receives data from the shipping layer to push it to a storage layer. It comes with the following features:

- Generally, the ingestion layer has a pluggable architecture to ease integration with the various sources of data and destinations, with the help of a set of plugins. Some of the plugins are made for receiving data from shippers, which means that data is not always received from shippers and can directly come from a data source, such as a file, network, or even a database. It can be ambiguous in some cases: should I use a shipper or a pipeline to ingest data from the file? It will obviously depend on the use case and also on the expected SLAs.

- The ingestion layer should be used to prepare the data by, for example, parsing the data, formatting the data, doing the correlation with other data sources, and normalizing and enriching the data before storage. This has many advantages, but the most important is that it can improve the quality of the data, providing better insights for visualization. Another advantage could be to remove processing overhead later on, by precomputing a value or looking up a reference. The drawback of this is that you may need to ingest the data again if the data is not properly formatted or enriched for visualization. Hopefully, there are some ways to process the data after it has been ingested.

- Ingesting and transforming data consumes compute resources. It is essential that we consider this, usually in terms of maximum data throughput per unit, and plan to ingestion by distributing the load over multiple ingestion instances. This is a very important aspect of real-time visualization which is, to be precise, near real-time. If ingestion is spread across multiple instances, it can accelerate the storage of the data, and therefore make it available faster for visualization.

Storing data at scale

Storage is undoubtedly the masterpiece of the data-driven architecture. It provides the essential, long-term retention of your data. It also provides the core functionality to search, analyze, and discover insights in your data. It is the heart of the process. The action will depend on the nature of the technology. Here are some aspects that the storage layer usually brings:

- Scalability is the main aspect, the storage used for various volumes of data which could start from GB, TB, to PB of data. The scalability is horizontal, which means that as the demand and volume grow, you should be able to increase the capacity of the storage seamlessly by adding more machines.

- Most of the time, a non-relational and highly distributed data store, which allows fast data access and analysis at a high volume and on a variety of data types, is used, namely a NoSQL data store. Data is partitioned and spread over a set of machines, in order to balance the load while reading or writing data.
- For data visualization, it's essential that the storage exposes an API to make analysis on top of the data. Letting the visualization layer do the statistical analysis, such as grouping data over a given dimension (aggregation), wouldn't scale.
- The nature of the API depends on the expectation on the visualization layer, but most of the time it's about aggregations. The visualization should only render the result of the heavy lifting done at the storage level.
- A data-driven architecture can serve data to a lot of different applications and users, and for different levels of SLAs. High availability becomes the norm in such architecture and, like scalability, it should be part of the nature of the solution.

Visualizing data

The visualization layer is the window on the data. It provides a set of tools to build live graphs and charts to bring the data to life, allowing you to build rich, insightful dashboards that answer the questions: What is happening now? Is my business healthy? What is the mood of the market?

The visualization layer in a data-driven architecture is one of the potential data consumers and is mostly focused on bringing KPIs on top of stored data. It comes with the following essential features:

- It should be lightweight and only render the result of processing done in the storage layer
- It allows the user to discover the data and get quick out-of-the box insights on the data
- It brings a visual way to ask unexpected questions to the data, rather than having to implement the proper request to do that
- In modern data architectures that must address the needs of accessing KPIs as fast as possible, the visualization layer should render the data in near real-time
- The visualization framework should be extensible and allow users to customize the existing assets or to add new features depending on the needs
- The user should be able to share the dashboards outside of the visualization application

As you can see, it's not only a matter of visualization. You need some foundations to reach the objectives.

This is how we'll address the use of Kibana in this book: we'll focus on use cases and see what is the best way to leverage Kibana features, depending on the use case and context.

The main differentiator with the other visualization tools is that Kibana comes along a full stack, the Elastic stack, with a seamless integration with every layer of the stack, which just eases the deployment of such architecture.

There are a lot of other technologies out there; we'll now see what they are good at and what their limits are.

Technologies limits

In this part, we'll try to analyze why some technologies can have limitations when trying to fulfill the expectations of a data-driven architecture.

Relational databases

I still come across people using relational databases to store their data in the context of a data-driven architecture; for example, in the use case of application monitoring, the logs are stored in MySQL. But when it comes to data visualization, it starts to break all the essential features we mentioned earlier:

- A **Relational Database Management System** (**RDBMS**) only manages fixed schemas and is not designed to deal with dynamic data models and unstructured data. Any structural changes made on the data will need to update the schema/tables, which, as everybody knows, is expensive.
- RDBMS doesn't allow real-time data access at scale. It wouldn't be realistic, for example, to create an index for each column for each table, for each schema in a RDBMS; but essentially that is what would be needed for real-time access.
- Scalability is not the easiest thing for RDBMS; it can be a complex and heavy process to put in place and wouldn't scale against a data explosion.

RDBMS should be used as a source of data that can be used before ingestion time to correlate or enrich ingested data to have a better granularity in the visualized data.

Visualization is about providing users with the flexibility to create multiple views of the data, enabling them to explore and ask their own questions without predefining a schema or constructing a view in the storage layer.

Hadoop

The Hadoop ecosystem is pretty rich in terms of projects. It's often hard to pick or understand which project will fit the ones needed; if we step back, we can consider the following aspects that Hadoop fulfills:

- It fits for massive-scale data architecture and will help to store and process any kind of data, for any level of volume
- It has out of-the-box batch and streaming technologies that will help to process the data as it comes in to create an iterative view on top of the raw data, or longer processing for larger-scale views
- The underlying architecture is made to make the integration of processing engines easy, so you can plug and process your data with a lot of different frameworks
- It's made to implement the data lake paradigms where one will essentially drop its data in order to process it

But what about visualization? Well, there are tons of initiatives out there, but the problem is that none of them can go against the real nature of Hadoop, which doesn't help for real-time data visualization at scale:

- Hadoop Distributed File System (HDFS) is a sequential read and write filesystem, which doesn't help for random access.
- Even the interactive ad hoc query or the existing real-time API doesn't scale in terms of integration with the visualization application. Most of the time, the user has to export its data outside of Hadoop in order to visualize it; some visualizations claim to have a transparent integration with HDFS, whereas under the hood, the data is exported and loaded in the memory in batches, which make the user experience pretty heavy and slow.
- Data visualization is all about APIs and easy access to the data, which Hadoop is not good at, as it always requires implementation from the user.

Hadoop is good for processing data, and is often used conjointly with other real-time technology, such as Elastic, to build Lambda architectures as shown in the following diagram:

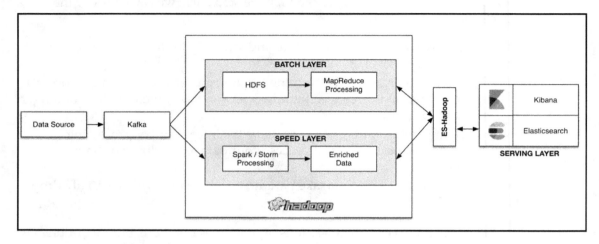

Lambda architecture with Elastic as a serving layer

In this architecture, you can see that Hadoop aggregates incoming data either in a long processing zone or a near real-time zone. Finally, the results are indexed in **Elasticsearch** in order to be visualized in **Kibana**. This means essentially that one technology is not meant to replace the other, but that you can leverage the best of both.

NoSQL

There are a lot of different very performant and massively scalable NoSQL technologies out there, such as key value stores, document stores, and columnar stores, but most of them do not serve analytic APIs or don't come with an out-of-the box visualization application.

In most cases, the data that these technologies is using is ingested in an indexation engine such as Elasticsearch to provide analytics capabilities for visualization or search purposes.

With the fundamental layers that a data-driven architecture should have and the limits identified in existing technologies in the market, let's now introduce the Elastic stack, which essentially answers these shortcomings.

Overview of the Elastic stack

The Elastic stack, formerly called ELK, provides the different layers that are needed to implement a data-driven architecture.

It starts from the ingestion layer with **Beats**, **Logstash**, and the **ES-Hadoop** connector, to a distributed data store with Elasticsearch, and finally to visualization with **Kibana**, as shown in the following figure:

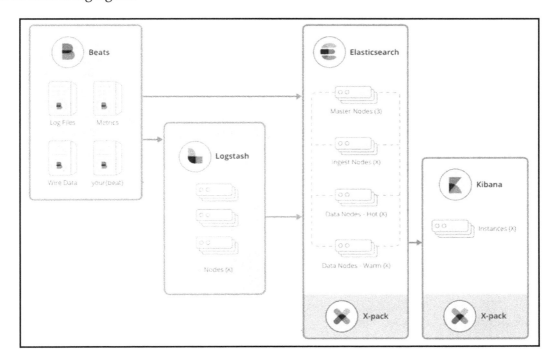

Elastic stack structure

As we can see in the diagram, Kibana is just one component of it.

In the following chapters, we'll focus in detail on how to use Kibana in different contexts, but we'll always need the other components. That's why you will need to understand the roles of each of them in this chapter.

One other important thing is that this book intends to describe how to use Kibana 5.0; thus, in this book, we'll use the Elastic stack 5.0.0 (https://www.elastic.co/blog/elastic-stack-5-0-0-released).

Elasticsearch

Elasticsearch is a distributed and scalable data store from which Kibana will pull out all the aggregation results that are used in the visualization. It's resilient by nature and is designed to scale out, which means that nodes can be added to an Elasticsearch cluster depending on the needs in a very simple way.

Elasticsearch is a highly available technology, which means that:

- First, data is replicated across the cluster so in case of failure there is still at least one copy of the data
- Secondly, thanks to its distributed nature, Elasticsearch can spread the indexing and searching load over the cluster nodes, to ensure service continuity and respect to your SLAs

It can deal with structured and unstructured data, and as we visualize data in Kibana, you will notice that data, or documents to use Elastic vocabulary, are indexed in the form of JSON documents. JSON makes it very handy to deal with complex data structures as it supports nested documents, arrays, and so on.

Elasticsearch is a developer-friendly solution and offers a large set of REST APIs to interact with the data, or the settings of the cluster itself. The documentation for these APIs can be found at `https://www.elastic.co/guide/en/elasticsearch/reference/current/docs.html`.

The parts that will be interesting for this book are mainly aggregations and graphs, which respectively will be used to make analytics on top of the indexed data (`https://www.elastic.co/guide/en/elasticsearch/reference/current/search-aggregations.html`) and create relations between documents (`https://www.elastic.co/guide/en/graph/current/graph-api-rest.html`).

On top of these APIs, there are also client APIs which allow Elasticsearch to be integrated with most technologies such as Java, Python, Go, and so on (`https://www.elastic.co/guide/en/elasticsearch/client/index.html`.).

Kibana generates the requests made to the cluster for each visualization. We'll see in this book how to dig into it and what features and APIs have been used.

The last main aspect for Elasticsearch is that it's a real-time technology that allows working with all ranges of volumes from gigabytes to petabytes, with the different APIs.

Besides Kibana, there are lot of different solutions that can leverage the open APIs that Elasticsearch offers to build visualization on top of the data; but Kibana is the only technology dedicated to it.

Beats

Beat is a lightweight data shipper which transports data from different sources such as applications, machines, or networks. Beats is built on top of **libbeat**, an open source library that allows every flavor of beat to send data to Elasticsearch, as illustrated in the following diagram:

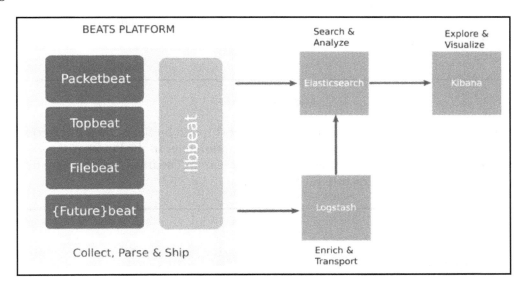

Beats architecture

The diagram shows the following Beats:

- **Packetbeat**, which essentially sniffs packets over the network wire for specific protocols such as MySQL and HTTP. It basically grabs all the fundamental metrics that will be used to monitor the protocol in question. For example, in the case of HTTP, it will get the request, the response, wrap into a document, and index it into Elasticsearch. We'll not use this beat in the book, as it would require a full book on it, so I encourage you to go on the following website to see what kind of Kibana dashboard you can build on top of it: http://demo.elastic.co.

- **Filebeat** is meant to securely transport the content of a file from point A to point B like the `tail` command. We'll use this beat jointly with the new ingest node (`ht tps://www.elastic.co/guide/en/elasticsearch/reference/master/ingest.html`) to push data from file directly to Elasticsearch, which will process the data before indexing it. The architecture can then be simplified, as shown in the following figure:

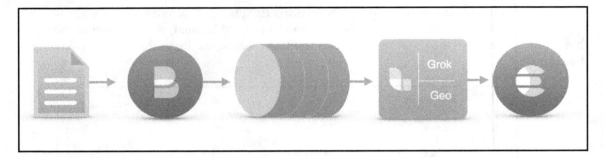

Ingestion pipeline without ingest

- In the preceding diagram, the data is first shipped by Beats, then put into a message broker (we'll come back to this notion later in the book), processed by Logstash, before being indexed by Elasticsearch. The ingest node dramatically simplifies the architecture for the use case:

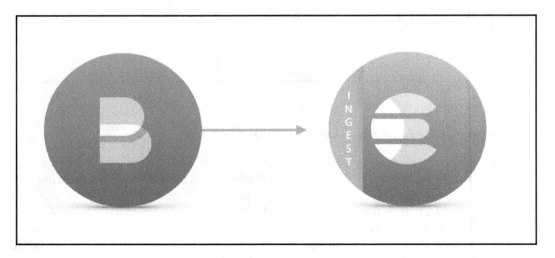

Ingestion pipeline with Ingest node

As the preceding diagrams show, the architecture is reduced to two components with filebeat and the ingest node. We'll be then able to visualize the content in Kibana.

- **Topbeat** is the first kind of Metricbeat that allows us to ship machines or application execution metrics to Elasticsearch. We'll also use it later on in this book to ship our laptop data and visualize it in Kibana. The good thing here is that this Beat comes with pre-built templates which only need to be imported in Kibana, as the document generated by the Beat is standard.
- There are a lot of different Beats made by the community that can be used for interesting data visualization. A list of them can be found at `https://www.elastic.co/guide/en/beats/libbeat/current/index.html`.

While Beats offer some basic filtering features, they don't provide the level of transformation that Logstash can bring.

Logstash

Logstash is a data processor that embraces the centralized data processing paradigm. It allows the users to collect, enrich/transform, and transport data to destinations with the help of more than 200 plugins, as shown in the following figure:

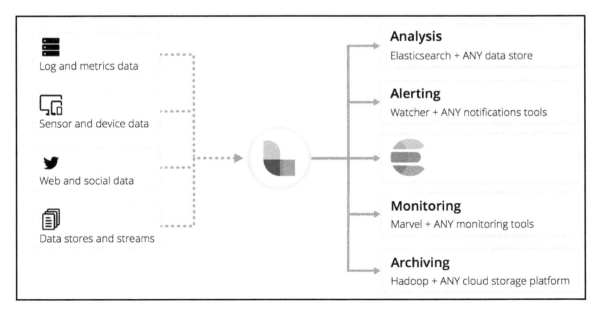

Logstash, the processing pipeline

Logstash is capable of collecting data from any source including Beats as every Beat comes with an out-of-the box integration for Logstash. The separation of roles is clear here: while beats is responsible for shipping the data, Logstash allows for processing the data before indexation.

From a data visualization point of view, Logstash should be used in order to prepare the data; we will see, for example, later in this book that you could receive IP addresses in logs from which it might be useful to deduce a geo-location. This can be done with the new geoip plugin, which is available at: `https://www.elastic.co/guide/en/logstash/curren t/plugins-filters-geoip.html`. This helps to get the following kind of visualization:

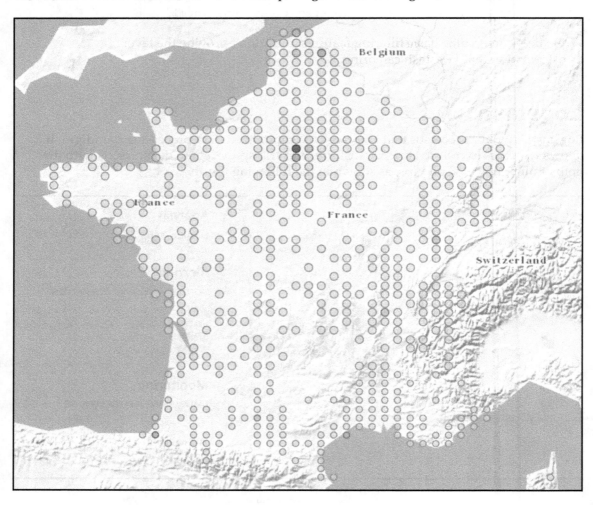

IP address visualization on a map

We'll see in our use cases how data preparation is important to comply with the different available visualizations in Kibana.

Kibana

Kibana is the core product described in this book; it's where all the user interface actions happen. Most of the visualization technology handles the analytical processing, whereas Kibana is just a web application that renders analytical processing done by Elasticsearch. It doesn't load data from Elasticsearch and then process it, but leverages the power of Elasticsearch to do all the heavy lifting. This basically allows real-time visualization at scale: as the data grows, the Elasticsearch cluster is scaled relatively to offer the best latency depending on the SLAs.

Kibana provides the visual power to Elasticsearch aggregations, allowing you to slice through your time-series datasets, or segment your data fields, as easy as pie.

Kibana is fitted for time-based visualization, even if your data can come without any timestamp, and brings visualization made for rendering the Elasticsearch aggregation framework. The following screenshot shows an example of a dashboard built in Kibana:

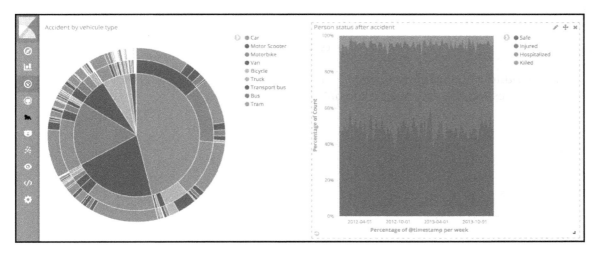

Kibana dashboard

As you can see, a dashboard contains one or more visualizations. We'll dig into them one by one in the context of our use cases. To build a dashboard, the user is brought into a data exploration experience where they will:

- Discover its data by digging into the indexed document as the following screenshot shows:

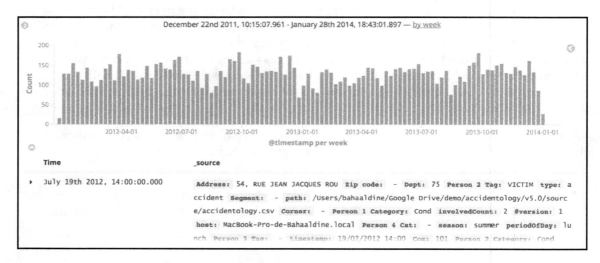

Discover data view

- Build visualizations with the help of a comprehensive palette, based on the question the user has for the data:

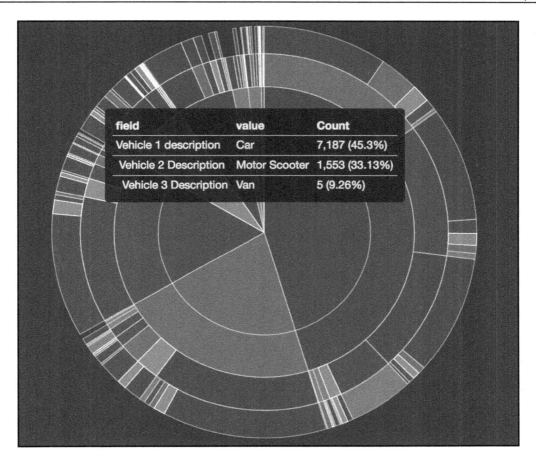

field	value	Count
Vehicle 1 description	Car	7,187 (45.3%)
Vehicle 2 Description	Motor Scooter	1,553 (33.13%)
Vehicle 3 Description	Van	5 (9.26%)

Kibana pie chart visualization

The preceding visualization shows the vehicles involved in an accident in Paris. In the example, the first vehicle was a **Car**, the second a **Motor Scooter**, and the last one a **Van**. We will dig into the accidentology dataset in the logging use case.

- Build an analytics experience by composing the different visualizations in a dashboard.

The plugin structure of Kibana makes it infinitely extensible. You'll see that Kibana is not only made for analytics on top of your data, but also to monitor your Elastic stack, build relations between documents, and also to do metrics analytics:

Kibana 5 plugin picker

X-Pack

Lastly I would like to introduce the concept of X-Pack, which will also be used in the book. While X-Pack is part of the subscription offer, one can download it on the Elastic website and use a trial license to evaluate it.

X-Pack is a set of plugins for Elasticsearch and Kibana that provides the following enterprise features.

Security

Security helps to secure the architecture at the data and access level. On the access side, the Elasticsearch cluster can be integrated with an LDAP, Active Directory, and PKI to enable role-based access on the cluster. There are additional ways to access it, either by what we call a native realm (https://www.elastic.co/guide/en/shield/current/native-realm.html), local to the cluster, or a custom realm (https://www.elastic.co/guide/en/shield/current/custom-realms.html), to integrate with other sources of authentication.

By adding role-based access to the cluster, users will only see data that they are allowed to see at the index level, document level, and field level.

From a data visualization point of view, this means, for example, that if a set of users are sharing data within the same index, but are for the first set only allowed to see French data, and for the other group only to see German data, they could both have a Kibana instance pointing to the index, but which, with the help of the underlying permissions configuration, renders the respective country data.

On the data side, the transport layer between Elasticsearch nodes can be encrypted. Transport can also be secured at the Elasticsearch and Kibana level, which means that the Kibana URL can be behind HTTPS.

Lastly, the security plugin provides IP filtering, but more importantly for data visualization, audit logging that tracks all the access to the cluster and can be easily rendered as a Kibana dashboard.

Monitoring

Monitoring is a Kibana plugin that gives insights on the infrastructure. While this was made primarily for Elasticsearch, Elastic is extending it for other parts of the architecture, such as Kibana or Logstash. That way, the users will have a single point of monitoring of all Elastic components and can track, for example, whether Kibana is executing properly, as shown in the following screenshot:

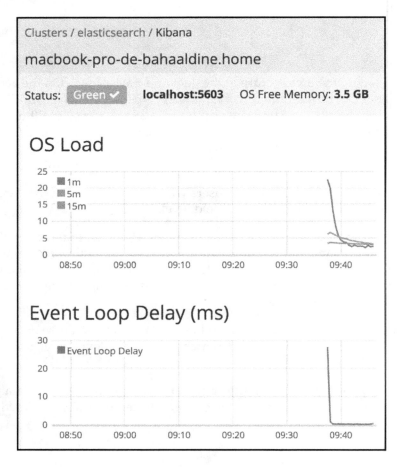

Kibana monitoring plugin

As you can see, users are able to see how many concurrent connections are made on Kibana, as well as deeper metrics such as the **Event Loop Delay**, which essentially represents the performance of the Kibana instance.

Alerting

If alerting is combined with monitoring data, it then enables proactive monitoring of both your Elasticinfra and your data. The alerting framework lets you describe queries to schedule and action in the background to define:

- When you want to run the alert; in other words, to schedule the execution of the alert
- What you want to watch by setting a condition that leverages Elasticsearch search, aggregations, and graph APIs
- What you want to do when the watch is triggered: write the result in a file, in an index, send it by e-mail, or send it over HTTP

The watch states are also indexed in Elasticsearch, which allows visualization to see the life cycle of the watch. Typically, you would render a graph that monitors certain metrics and the related triggered watches as shown in the following diagram:

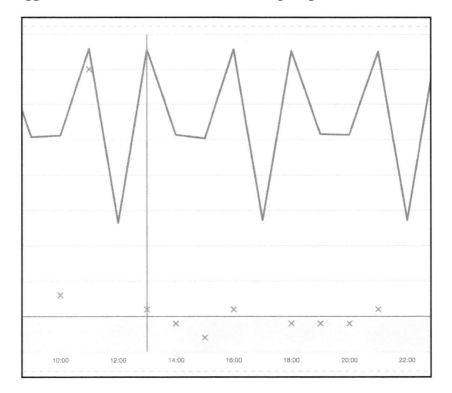

Alerts shown on a visualization

The important aspect of the preceding visualization is that the user can see when the alerts have been triggered and how many of them, depending on a threshold.

We will use alerting later in this book in a metric analytics use case based on the performance of the CPU.

Graph

Graph is probably one of the most exciting features of the version 2.3 release at the beginning of 2016. It provides both an API and a plugin for visualization in Kibana, and brings the ability to build relations between documents indexed in Elasticsearch. Unlike what lots of users think, graph is not a graph database; it actually redefines what graph is and seeks for relevant relations between data based on a relevancy ranking, regardless of how the data has been modeled from the start.

Figuring out the frequency of a term in the background dataset is what the search engines naturally understand when they do relevancy ranking; they know how common a word is.

When we throw terms in the Elasticsearch indices, it naturally knows which things are the most interesting, and this logic is applied to the graph.

The easiest way to use graph is to start in Kibana with the help of the graph plugin, and explore the data, as the following figure shows:

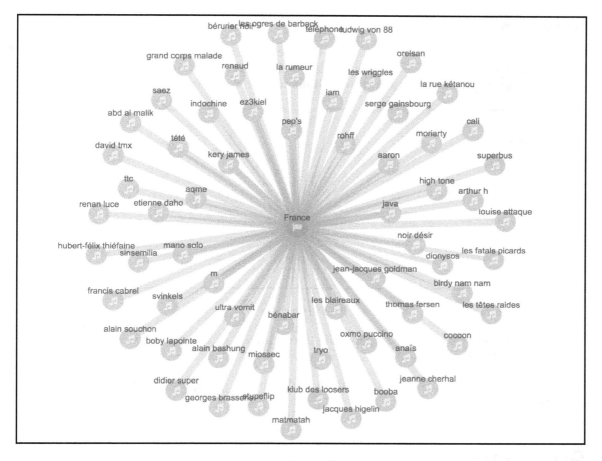

Graph visualization in Kibana

In this graph, we can see a country, France, and all the related artists based on the music dataset.

We'll use graph in the related use case later in this book.

Reporting

Reporting is a new plugin brought in with the latest 2.x version to allow users to export the Kibana dashboard as a PDF. This is one of the most expected features from the Kibana users and is as simple as clicking on a button, as illustrated in the following screenshot:

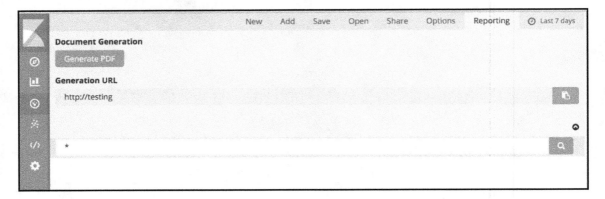

PDF generation in Kibana

The PDF generation is put into a queue; the users can follow the export process, and then download the PDF.

In the following chapter, we will get started with Kibana, going through the installation and a complete first use guide.

Summary

At this point, you should have a clear view of the different required components to build up a data-driven architecture. We have also seen how the Elastic stack fits this need, and that Kibana requires the other components of the stack in order to ship, transform, and store the visualized data.

In the next chapter, we'll see how to get started with Kibana and install all the components you need to see your first dashboard.

2
Installing and Setting Up Kibana 5.0

In this chapter, we'll go through all the installation steps required to use Kibana. At the time of writing, version 5.0 has not yet been released; however, Elastic's terrific R&D team will bring to the user a pre-release of the major version in the form of an alpha or beta version. Therefore, I'm able to use the 5.0.0-alpha4 version to illustrate the majority of what you will get in 5.0.

Setting up Kibana 5.0 also requires that you set up Elasticsearch as well, configuring security in order to integrate Elasticsearch and Kibana, as shown in the following diagram:

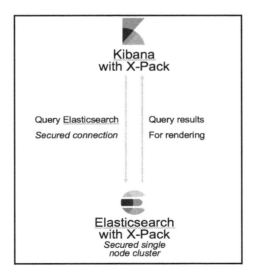

Kibana and Elasticsearch integration

Setting up your installation

In this section, we'll download and install Elasticsearch, Kibana, and the X-Pack.

Downloading the software

Downloading the binaries is pretty straightforward; you just need to get on the Elastic website on the following pages:

- For Elasticsearch: `https://www.elastic.co/downloads/elasticsearch`. On this page, you will find the current GA version, which might be a 5.x by the time you read this book. In my case, I'll download **5.0.0-alpha4**:

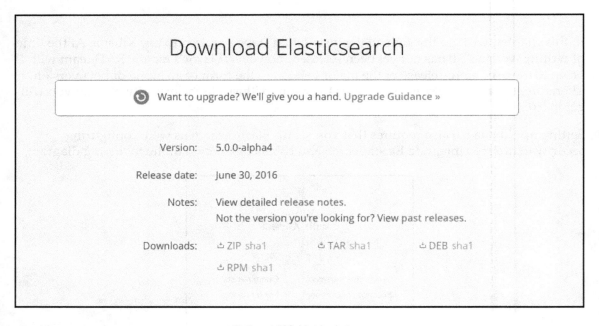

Elasticsearch 5.0.0-alpha4 download page

- For Kibana: `https://www.elastic.co/downloads/kibana`. As for Elasticsearch, I'm going to download **5.0.0-alpha4**:

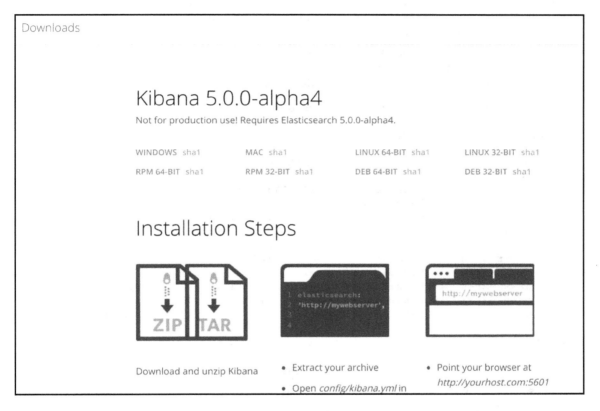

Kibana 5.0.0-alpha4 download page

I recommend that you move the downloaded file to the same folder. In my case, I've moved everything to the `/Users/Bahaaldine/packt` folder:

```
pc55:packt bahaaldine$ pwd
/Users/bahaaldine/packt
pc55:packt bahaaldine$ ls
elasticsearch-5.0.0-alpha4.tar.gz  kibana-5.0.0-alpha4-darwin-
  x64.tar.gz
```

You can now proceed to both Elasticsearch and Kibana installation.

Installing Elasticsearch

Installing Elasticsearch is mandatory to use Kibana. As demonstrated previously, Elasticsearch is a data store that exposes data through a variety of APIs (search, aggregation, and graphs). Kibana relies on Elasticsearch to render the data into a graph; it sends queries to Elasticsearch, such as aggregation queries, and displays the result sent back by Elasticsearch in charts. Elasticsearch is the unique data source that Kibana supports. The installation step is as easy as unzipping the downloaded archive:

```
pc55:packt bahaaldine$ tar -zxvf elasticsearch-5.0.0-alpha4.tar.gz
```

The resulting uncompressed folder is structured as follows:

```
pc55:elasticsearch-5.0.0-alpha4 bahaaldine$ ls -l
total 56
-rw-r--r--@  1 bahaaldine  wheel  11358 27 jan 13:53 LICENSE.txt
-rw-r--r--@  1 bahaaldine  wheel    150 21 jui 16:55 NOTICE.txt
-rw-r--r--@  1 bahaaldine  wheel   9129 21 jui 16:55 README.textile
drwxr-xr-x@ 14 bahaaldine  wheel    476  5 jul 13:51 bin
drwxr-xr-x@  7 bahaaldine  wheel    238  5 jul 13:51 config
drwxr-xr-x   3 bahaaldine  wheel    102  5 jul 13:51 data
drwxr-xr-x@ 35 bahaaldine  wheel   1190 27 jui 18:26 lib
drwxr-xr-x  16 bahaaldine  wheel    544 14 jul 02:22 logs
drwxr-xr-x@ 10 bahaaldine  wheel    340 27 jui 18:26 modules
drwxr-xr-x   3 bahaaldine  wheel    102  5 jul 13:51 plugins
```

It is worth explaining what some of the preceding folder contains:

- The `bin` directory contains Elasticsearch executable files
- `Config` will contain not only the Elasticsearch node configuration but also all eventual plugin files
- `Data` will contain all the data indexed in the Elasticsearch node

As you can see, as described in the diagram at the beginning of this chapter, this is our single-node Elasticsearch cluster installation folder. In this book, we'll just create a single Elasticsearch node cluster, as the focus is Kibana rather than Elasticsearch cluster configuration. You can, however, install new nodes and apply the same configuration to them if you want to.

To check your installation, we'll need to run Elasticsearch and see whether everything is running correctly. By everything, I mean in terms of execution, but also in terms of access. Go to your installation folder:

```
pc55:bin bahaaldine$ pwd
/Users/bahaaldine/packt/elasticsearch-5.0.0-alpha4/bin
```

Now start Elasticsearch with the following command:

```
pc55:bin bahaaldine$ ./elasticsearch
[2016-07-15 23:10:35,773][INFO ][node] [Pasco] version[5.0.0-alpha4],
pid[64920], build[3f5b994/2016-06-27T16:23:46.861Z], OS[Mac OS
X/10.11.5/x86_64], JVM[Oracle Corporation/Java HotSpot(TM) 64-Bit Server
VM/1.8.0_91/25.91-b14]
[2016-07-15 23:10:35,774][INFO ][node] [Pasco] initializing ...
[2016-07-15 23:10:36,668][INFO ][plugins] [Pasco] modules [percolator,
lang-mustache, lang-painless, reindex, aggs-matrix-stats, lang-expression,
ingest-common, lang-groovy], plugins []
[2016-07-15 23:10:37,475][INFO ][env] [Pasco] using [1] data paths,
mounts [[/ (/dev/disk1)]], net usable_space [166gb], net total_space
[464.7gb], spins? [unknown], types [hfs]
[2016-07-15 23:10:37,476][INFO ][env] [Pasco] heap size [1.9gb],
compressed ordinary object pointers [true]
[2016-07-15 23:10:39,001][INFO ][node] [Pasco] initialized
[2016-07-15 23:10:39,002][INFO ][node] [Pasco] starting ...
[2016-07-15 23:10:39,133][INFO ][transport] [Pasco] publish_address
{127.0.0.1:9300}, bound_addresses {[fe80::1]:9300}, {[::1]:9300},
{127.0.0.1:9300}
[2016-07-15 23:10:39,139][WARN ][bootstrap] [Pasco] initial heap size
[268435456] not equal to maximum heap size [2147483648]; this can cause
resize pauses and prevents mlockall from locking the entire heap
[2016-07-15 23:10:39,139][WARN ][bootstrap] [Pasco] please set
[discovery.zen.minimum_master_nodes] to a majority of the number of master
eligible nodes in your cluster
[2016-07-15 23:10:42,199][INFO ][cluster.service] [Pasco] new_master
{Pasco}{zv3EKSi_TqCvA_lJkByphw}{127.0.0.1}{127.0.0.1:9300}, reason: zen-
disco-join(elected_as_master, [0] nodes joined)
[2016-07-15 23:10:42,215][INFO ][http] [Pasco] publish_address
{127.0.0.1:9200}, bound_addresses {[fe80::1]:9200}, {[::1]:9200},
{127.0.0.1:9200}
[2016-07-15 23:10:42,215][INFO ][node] [Pasco] started
[2016-07-15 23:10:42,231][INFO ][gateway] [Pasco] recovered [0] indices
into cluster_state
```

The preceding logs are what you should get when you start Elasticsearch for the first time.

 If you are having trouble installing it, it may be because of your local system configuration. I then recommend that you refer to the installation documentation: `https://www.elastic.co/guide/en/elasticsearch/re` `ference/master/install-elasticsearch.html`.

If you open a web browser and go to `http://localhost:9200/`, you should get the following JSON output:

```
{
  name: "Pasco",
  cluster_name: "elasticsearch",
  version: {
  number: "5.0.0-alpha4",
    build_hash: "3f5b994",
    build_date: "2016-06-27T16:23:46.861Z",
    build_snapshot: false,
    lucene_version: "6.1.0"
  },
  tagline: "You Know, for Search"
}
```

This JSON document indicates that the service is up and responding to API requests, and provides details regarding the version and build of your Elasticsearch instance, such as the node name, here, `Pasco`, and the version number, here, `5.0.0-alpha4`.

Installing Kibana

Kibana default installation is as simple as downloading the archive file and opening it in the desired directory location. Start by uncompressing the `Kibana` folder:

```
pc55:packt bahaaldine$ tar -zxvf kibana-4.5.3-darwin-x64.tar.gz
```

The directory structure is as follows:

```
pc55:kibana-5.0.0-alpha4-darwin-x64 bahaaldine$ ls -l
total 24
-rw-r--r--@  1 bahaaldine  staff   563 29 jui 19:55 LICENSE.txt
-rw-r--r--@  1 bahaaldine  staff  2445 29 jui 19:55 README.txt
drwxr-xr-x@  4 bahaaldine  staff   136 29 jui 19:55 bin
drwxr-xr-x@  3 bahaaldine  staff   102 29 jui 19:55 config
drwxr-xr-x@  3 bahaaldine  staff   102 29 jui 19:55
installedPlugins
drwxr-xr-x@  9 bahaaldine  staff   306 29 jui 19:55 node
```

```
drwxr-xr-x@ 95 bahaaldine   staff   3230 29 jui 19:55 node_modules
drwxr-xr-x@  4 bahaaldine   staff    136 29 jui 19:55 optimize
-rw-r--r--@  1 bahaaldine   staff    708 29 jui 19:55 package.json
drwxr-xr-x@  9 bahaaldine   staff    306 29 jui 19:55 src
drwxr-xr-x@ 15 bahaaldine   staff    510 29 jui 19:55 webpackShims
```

You only have to worry about the `bin` and `config` directories, which respectively contain the Kibana binaries and the `configuration` file. In Chapter 9, *Creating a Custom Plugin For Kibana 5.0*, we'll see that some of the others need attention as well. Make sure Elasticsearch is still running and check your installation by running Kibana:

```
pc55:bin bahaaldine$ pwd
/Users/bahaaldine/packt/kibana-5.0.0-alpha4-darwin-x64/bin
pc55:bin bahaaldine$ ./kibana
```

You should get the following logs:

```
    log   [08:49:50.648] [info][status][plugin:kibana@1.0.0] Status changed
from uninitialized to green - Ready
    log   [08:49:50.669] [info][status][plugin:elasticsearch@1.0.0]
Status changed from uninitialized to yellow - Waiting for Elasticsearch
    log   [08:49:50.685] [info][status][plugin:console@1.0.0] Status
changed from uninitialized to green - Ready
    log   [08:49:50.697] [info][status][plugin:kbn_doc_views@1.0.0]
Status changed from uninitialized to green - Ready
    log   [08:49:50.699]
[info][status][plugin:kbn_vislib_vis_types@1.0.0] Status changed from
uninitialized to green - Ready
    log   [08:49:50.703] [info][status][plugin:markdown_vis@1.0.0] Status
changed from uninitialized to green - Ready
    log   [08:49:50.707] [info][status][plugin:metric_vis@1.0.0] Status
changed from uninitialized to green - Ready
    log   [08:49:50.709] [info][status][plugin:spy_modes@1.0.0] Status
changed from uninitialized to green - Ready
    log   [08:49:50.713] [info][status][plugin:status_page@1.0.0] Status
changed from uninitialized to green - Ready
    log   [08:49:50.716] [info][status][plugin:table_vis@1.0.0] Status
changed from uninitialized to green - Ready
    log   [08:49:50.720] [info][listening] Server running at
http://0.0.0.0:5601
    log   [08:49:50.721] [info][status][ui settings] Status changed from
uninitialized to yellow - Elasticsearch plugin is yellow
    log   [08:49:55.751] [info][status][plugin:elasticsearch@1.0.0]
Status changed from yellow to yellow - No existing Kibana index found
    log   [08:49:56.293] [info][status][plugin:elasticsearch@1.0.0]
Status changed from yellow to green - Kibana index ready
    log   [08:49:56.294] [info][status][ui settings] Status changed from
yellow to green - Ready
```

The logs show Kibana starting up, validating connection with Elasticsearch, and, finally, turning to a green health status.

Well done! You've just successfully installed Elasticsearch and Kibana!

Kibana is running and you can get more information by opening a web browser and going to `http://localhost:5601/status`:

localhost:5601/status		
Status: Green		pc55.home

Heap Total (MB) 84.27	Heap Used (MB) 63.12	Load 1.55, 1.73, 1.84
Response Time Avg (ms) 0.00	Response Time Max (ms) 0.00	Requests Per Second 0.00

Status Breakdown

ID	Status
ui settings	✓ Ready
plugin:kibana@1.0.0	✓ Ready
plugin:elasticsearch@1.0.0	✓ Kibana index ready
plugin:console@1.0.0	✓ Ready
plugin:kbn_doc_views@1.0.0	✓ Ready
plugin:kbn_vislib_vis_types@1.0.0	✓ Ready
plugin:markdown_vis@1.0.0	✓ Ready
plugin:metric_vis@1.0.0	✓ Ready
plugin:spy_modes@1.0.0	✓ Ready
plugin:status_page@1.0.0	✓ Ready
plugin:table_vis@1.0.0	✓ Ready

Kibana status page

The status section provides an overview of the various components running within Kibana together with their health. Here you can see Kibana UI, Elasticsearch, and others, all reporting **Ready**.

Now that your Elasticsearch and Kibana installation is operating, we will install additional plugins, first X-Packs, and then Timelion.

Installing X-Packs

As mentioned previously, X-Packs is part of the subscription, and brings an additional set of enterprise features to Elasticstack, as shown in the following diagram:

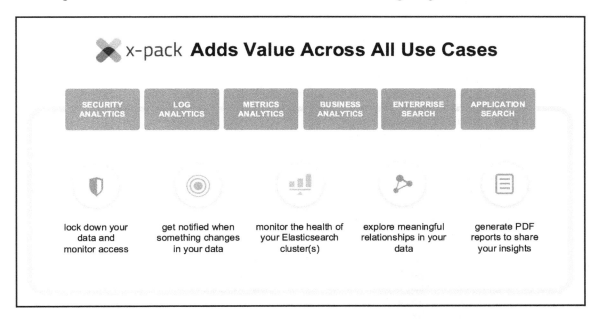

X-Packs structure

In this book, we will use all of them, as they provide very interesting features, such as authentication, monitoring, graph exploration, or PDF export, to the whole stack.

As a reminder, plugins exist at every level of the stack, whether it's Logstash, Kibana, or Elasticsearch. You can easily extend the product by implementing your own feature. Furthermore, each product comes with a command-line tool to enable plugin installation. Finally, while some plugins can only add features to one part of the stack, X-Pack aims to add plugins across the stack. For example, X-Pack brings a new API in Elasticsearch, but also new Kibana visualizations.

X-Packs needs to be installed both on Elasticsearch and Kibana in order to run. Let's start with Elasticsearch, by going into the relative home directory and running the following command:

WARNING: Plugin requires additional permissions

```
pc55:elasticsearch-5.0.0-alpha4 bahaaldine$ pwd
/Users/bahaaldine/packt/elasticsearch-5.0.0-alpha4
pc55:elasticsearch-5.0.0-alpha4 bahaaldine$ bin/elasticsearch-
plugin install x-pack
-> Downloading x-pack from elastic
* java.lang.RuntimePermission
accessClassInPackage.com.sun.activation.registries
* java.lang.RuntimePermission getClassLoader
* java.lang.RuntimePermission setContextClassLoader
* java.lang.RuntimePermission setFactory
* java.security.SecurityPermission createPolicy.JavaPolicy
* java.security.SecurityPermission getPolicy
* java.security.SecurityPermission putProviderProperty.BC
* java.security.SecurityPermission setPolicy
* java.util.PropertyPermission * read,write
* javax.net.ssl.SSLPermission setHostnameVerifier
Continue with installation? [y/N]y
-> Installed x-pack
```

See here for descriptions of what these permissions allow and the associated risks: http://docs.oracle.com/javase/8/docs/technotes/g uides/security/permissions.html.

```
    [2016-07-16 10:45:10,682][INFO ][cluster.metadata] [Scott Summers]
[.monitoring-data-2] creating index, cause [auto(bulk api)], templates
[.monitoring-data-2], shards [1]/[1], mappings [node, cluster_info, kibana]
    [2016-07-16 10:45:10,721][INFO ][cluster.metadata] [Scott Summers]
[.monitoring-es-2-2016.07.16] creating index, cause [auto(bulk api)],
templates [.monitoring-es-2], shards [1]/[1], mappings [node, shards,
_default_, index_stats, index_recovery, cluster_state, cluster_stats,
indices_stats, node_stats]
```

X-pack will now be securing Elasticsearch, and has automatically installed a set of default user profiles to get started with. This means all communication with the Elasticsearch API endpoints now require you to authenticate. You can see this by browsing to `http://localhost:9200`; an authentication popup will appear asking for a username and a password:

Authentication popup

My local browser is French, therefore I'm presented with a French login screen. You can easily see here that you have to provide credentials in order to display the go-through. The default username/password are `elastic`/`changeme`. These are automatically created by the security plugin provided by X-Packs.

If you want to tweak security, I recommend that you refer to the following documentation: `https://www.elastic.co/guide/en/x-pack/current/security-getting-started.html`.

Still in your browser, try to access the following URL with the preceding credentials: `http://localhost:9200/_xpack`.

You should get a JSON output giving the description of the installed X-Pack:

```json
{
    "build": {
        "hash": "bb03240",
        "date": "2016-06-27T16:26:32.109Z"
    },
    "license": {
        "uid": "d9afa57e-87b1-4bcc-9190-e6ca9f4f437e",
        "type": "trial",
        "mode": "trial",
        "status": "active",
        "expiry_date_in_millis": 1471250705138
    },
    "features": {
        "graph": {
            "description": "Graph Data Exploration for the Elastic
                Stack",
            "available": true,
            "enabled": true
        },
        "monitoring": {
            "description": "Monitoring for the Elastic Stack",
            "available": true,
            "enabled": true
        },
        "security": {
            "description": "Security for the Elastic Stack",
            "available": true,
            "enabled": true
        },
        "watcher": {
            "description": "Alerting, Notification and Automation for
                the Elastic Stack",
            "available": true,
            "enabled": true
        }
    },
    "tagline": "You know, for X"
}
```

The preceding shows what your X-Packs contains, the license type, and the expiration time.

We will now install X-Packs for Kibana by running the following command in the Kibana installation folder:

```
cpc55:bin bahaaldine$ pwd
/Users/bahaaldine/packt/kibana-5.0.0-alpha4-darwin-x64
pc55:kibana-5.0.0-alpha4-darwin-x64 bahaaldine$ bin/kibana-plugin
install x-pack
Attempting to transfer from x-pack
Attempting to transfer from https://download.elastic.co/kibana/x-
pack/x-pack-5.0.0-alpha4.zip
Transferring 60685004 bytes....................
Transfer complete
Retrieving metadata from plugin archive
Extracting plugin archive
Extraction complete
Optimizing and caching browser bundles...
Plugin installation complete
```

You should get the preceding installation logs.

Configuring security

There are a few points to consider in terms of security with Kibana: the first is to ensure that Kibana exposes an HTTPS endpoint to secure the connection to the UI; another is to encrypt the transport using the encryption key, and the last is to connect to Elasticsearch through certificates.

If you restart Kibana, you will see the following warning in the startup logs:

```
log     [11:21:32.024] [warning][security] Generating a random key for
xpack.security.encryptionKey. To prevent sessions from being invalidated on
restart, please set xpack.security.encryptionKey in kibana.yml
log     [11:21:32.027] [warning][security] Session cookies will be
transmitted over insecure connections. This is not recommended.
```

The first security warning can be solved by adding an encryption key to your Kibana configuration, in conf/kibana.yml. To get started, let's add a key value. In a production scenario, we would most likely pass the key as an environment variable or the like:

```
xpack.security.encryptionKey: "myEncryptionKey"
```

The second warning is about the connection, which is unsecured by default; in other words, not behind SSL. By default, X-Packs security provides the necessary configuration to enable TLS and SSL, but if you need to, you can provide .crt and .key files; you can easily generate them using the following command line, in the Kibana installation folder:

```
pc55:kibana-5.0.0-alpha4-darwin-x64 bahaaldine$ openssl req -x509  -batch -
nodes -newkey rsa:2048 -keyout kibana.key -out kibana.crt -subj
/CN=localhost
```

Then, edit the Kibana configuration file again and change the default settings to point to your new generated files, as shown in the following example:

```
# Paths to the PEM-format SSL certificate and SSL key files,
respectively. These
# files enable SSL for outgoing requests from the Kibana server to
the browser.
server.ssl.cert: /Users/bahaaldine/packt/kibana-5.0.0-alpha4-
darwin-x64/kibana.crt
server.ssl.key: /Users/bahaaldine/packt/kibana-5.0.0-alpha4-darwin-
x64/kibana.key
```

Now if you restart Kibana, all the warnings should have disappeared.

To connect to Elasticsearch using a certificate, you will first need to configure Elasticsearch to use certificates (https://www.elastic.co/guid e/en/x-pack/5.1/ssl-tls.html#enable-ssl), and then tell Kibana to connect to Elasticsearch using HTTPS (https://www.elastic.co/guide/e n/x-pack/5.1/kibana.html#configure-kibana-ssl).

Kibana anatomy

In this section, I'll present the different sections present in Kibana 5.0, without necessarily diving into them, as we are going to do this later in the chapters dedicated to logging, metrics, and graphs.

First, connect to `https://localhost:5601`, log in with the default `elastic`/`changeme`, and let's see what the Kibana menu is composed of:

Kibana menu

The Kibana menu contains two types of sections:

- Links to Kibana core features: **Discover**, **Visualize**, **Dashboard**, and **Console**
- Links to Kibana plugins: **Timelion**, **Graph**, **Monitoring**, the **elastic** user, and **Logout**

Before we start, let's go into a common Kibana user experience:

Kibana user experience

Since Kibana 5.0, the user can have a seamless experience, from ingestion to visualization, all from Kibana itself:

- If the user doesn't have data yet, he can import it using the CSV importer (only available in Kibana alpha version; has been removed in 5.0 GA).
- If the data already exists in Elasticsearch, the user needs to create their index patterns. The concept of index patterns describes a meta-structure on top of the actual index structure, which is only used by Kibana to abstract the data layer. By doing so, Kibana allows customization, which will have no effect on the data layer, but only on the visualization layer.
- Then, the user discovers their data in the **Discover** tab, and sees which terms and metrics can be used as part of the visualization. The Discover tab allows a user to query and filter data through UI components, allowing a user to create data views, which they can save and give a name.
- Following that, the visualization tab allows the user to select a visualization type to display the data, essentially providing you with a toll to ask questions and display patterns.
- All the questions are then put together in a dashboard by drag and drop from a list of saved visualizations; the visualization experience starts from there.
- Other features of visualizations are provided by the plugins, such as **Graph** and Timelion.

We'll now look at Kibana's core features one by one.

Core components

In this section, we will go through Kibana's core components; in other words, components that are part of the out-of-the-box experience.

Discover

The Discover section is the first place you will go once you have indexed some data in Elasticsearch, in order to explore your data:

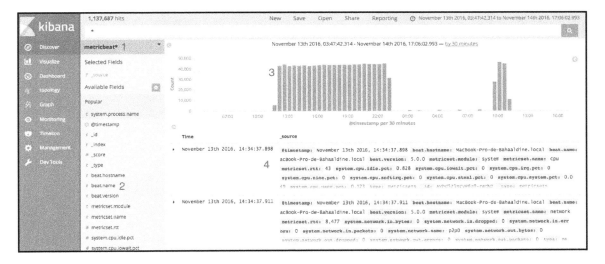

Kibana discover section

It shows the following:

1. Your index patterns (we will come back to this notion later), here, `metricbeats-*`.

2. The fields that exist within your index. Clicking on the field name, provides a simulation of the top values in that field. You can, for example, get a sneak peek of the process-name breakdown if you click on the `system.process.name` field in the available fields:

Process-name breakdown

3. The number of events across time in the form of a date histogram. The period is set with the time picker in the top-right corner.

4. The indexed document. If you expand one item, you will see a detailed description of the document:

Time	_source
▾ July 13th 2016, 10:50:07.492	**@timestamp**: July 13th 2016, 10:50:07.492 **beat.hostname**: MacBook-Pro-de-Bahaaldine.local **beat.name**: MacBook-Pro-de-Bahaaldine.local **metricset.module**: system **metricset.name**: memory **metricset.rtt**: 2,051 **system.memory.actual.free**: 5,57 5,241,728 **system.memory.actual.used.bytes**: 10.808GB **system.memory.actual. used.pct**: 67.55% system.memory.free: 1.241GB system.memory.swap.free: 1,112,

Link to /metricbeat-2016.07.13/metricsets/AVXjcuxCzpFg4rY7i6v3

Table   JSON

⊙ @timestamp	🔍 🔍 ☐ ✳	July 13th 2016, 10:50:07.492
t _id	🔍 🔍 ☐ ✳	AVXjcuxCzpFg4rY7i6v3
t _index	🔍 🔍 ☐ ✳	metricbeat-2016.07.13
# _score	🔍 🔍 ☐ ✳	2
t _type	🔍 🔍 ☐ ✳	metricsets
t beat.hostname	🔍 🔍 ☐ ✳	MacBook-Pro-de-Bahaaldine.local
t beat.name	🔍 🔍 ☐ ✳	MacBook-Pro-de-Bahaaldine.local
t metricset.module	🔍 🔍 ☐ ✳	system
t metricset.name	🔍 🔍 ☐ ✳	memory
# metricset.rtt	🔍 🔍 ☐ ✳	2,051
# system.memory.actual.free	🔍 🔍 ☐ ✳	5,575,241,728
# system.memory.actual.used.bytes	🔍 🔍 ☐ ✳	10.808GB
# system.memory.actual.used.pct	🔍 🔍 ☐ ✳	67.55%
# system.memory.free	🔍 🔍 ☐ ✳	1.241GB
# system.memory.swap.free	🔍 🔍 ☐ ✳	1,112,014,848
# system.memory.swap.total	🔍 🔍 ☐ ✳	4,294,967,296
# system.memory.swap.used.bytes	🔍 🔍 ☐ ✳	2.964GB
# system.memory.swap.used.pct	🔍 🔍 ☐ ✳	74.11%
# system.memory.total	🔍 🔍 ☐ ✳	16GB
# system.memory.used.bytes	🔍 🔍 ☐ ✳	14.759GB
# system.memory.used.pct	🔍 🔍 ☐ ✳	92.24%
t type	🔍 🔍 ☐ ✳	metricsets

Example of indexed document

You can see here a document created by MetricBeat, which collects and puts together the execution metrics from my MacBook, such as the system memory. We will see what Metricbeat is and how to visualize the data in detail in `Chapter 5`, *Metric Analytics with Metricbeat and Kibana 5.0*. From there, the common use of Kibana is to build visualizations in the **Visualize** section.

Visualize

The **Visualize** section is the place to build visualizations on top of the data you have indexed. It offers a palette of visualizations, as shown in the following screenshot:

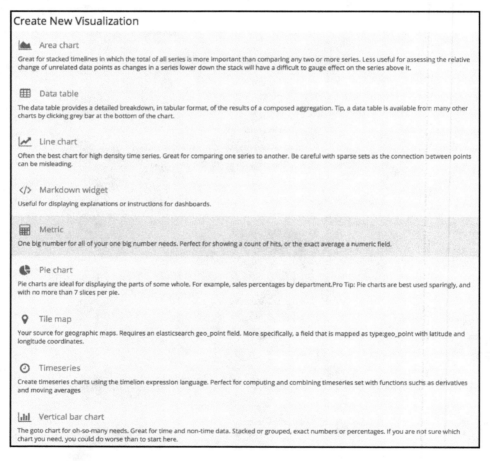

Kibana available visualizations

We will use all of them in the following chapters, but it is worth mentioning here the brand new **Timeseries** visualization, which brings Timelion visualization to a regular Kibana dashboard.

Also, if you already have saved a visualization and you want to modify it, you will now find it at the bottom of the same screen:

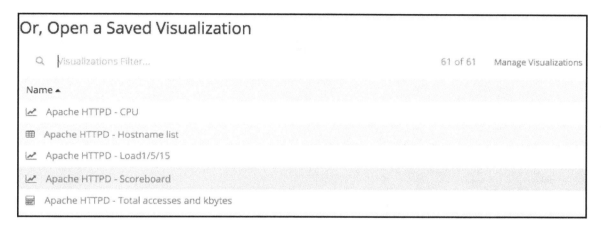

Saved visualization

Once you have your visualizations built, the common practice is to compose a dashboard.

Dashboard

In this section, you will be able to build a dashboard that puts together the visualizations built earlier, such as the following:

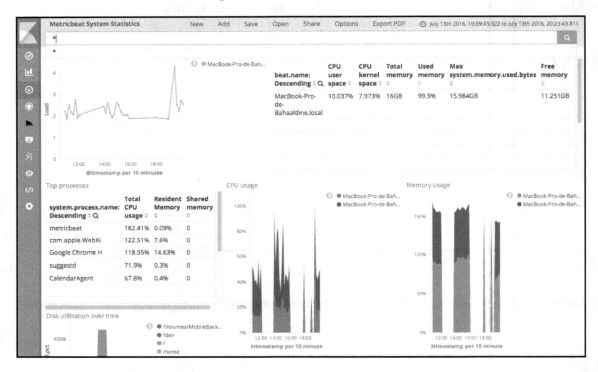

Kibana dashboard example

This example shows a dashboard built on top of the data collected by MetricBeat. We will see later in this book how easy it is to achieve these results using the out-of-the-box dashboards provided in the MetricBeat installation.

The Kibana dashboard in 5.0 is getting more space, as a lot of unused blocks have been removed, which gives a wider visualization experience to the user. Colors have been also streamlined and, let's say, modernized.

You can create, save, and open an existing dashboard, and even share them as in the previous versions of Kibana in the form of a link or an iFrame to be integrated in an existing portal. It's worth mentioning the new **Export PDF** option that we'll use later, which lets you export dashboards in PDF files.

Timelion

Timelion is the metric analytics visualization component of Timelion. The experience you get in Timelion of building visualizations is completely different than in Kibana visualization: it's expression-based. The user can build statistics on time-series data by combining expressions that either fetch data from one or more data sources, or apply mathematical functions on them. The result of the expression is a highly customizable visualization:

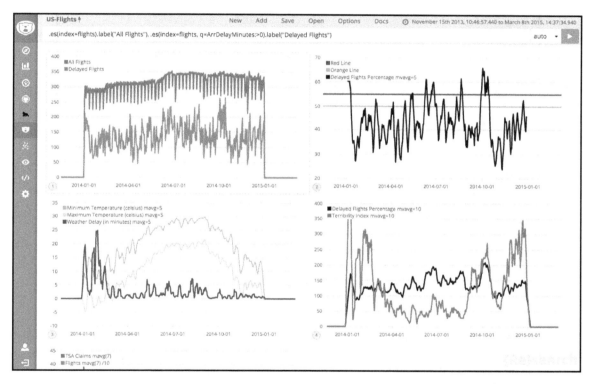

Timelion visualizations

The example shows the visualization we will build later in this book, for United States domestic flights. As you can see, Timelion has an expression bar, which provides an API to build visualizations. We will also look at how to use external data sources, which again is not something you can do in Kibana visualization.

Management

The **Management** section, formerly known as the **settings** section, contains all the management options for data, Elasticsearch, and Kibana, as shown in the following screenshot:

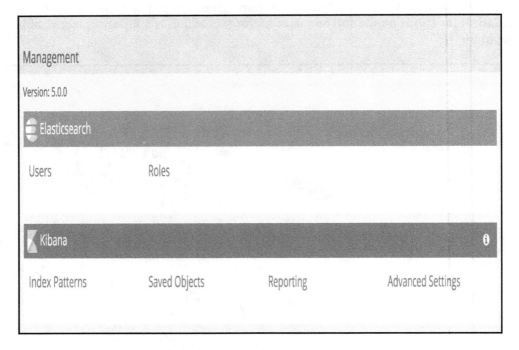

Kibana management section

With X-Packs installed, you also get an **Elasticsearch** panel to manage access via roles and users. Finally, all related Kibana settings are also listed here, such as managing the index patterns, the Kibana objects (visualizations, searches, and dashboards), reporting, which also comes with X-Packs, and the **Advanceds settings**.

DevTools/Console

DevTools regroups the tools that Elasticsearch developers will need, to test and optimize their Elasticsearch queries. As of version 5.1.1, it contains two features: Console, as part of the core Kibana, and Profiler UI, as part of X-Packs basic (free license), which I'll address in the following Plugins paragraph.

Console, formerly called Sense, is an Elasticsearch query console:

Console query example

The preceding example shows a query built with the help of the autocomplete feature in Console, which basically searches for documents that have the `system.process.name` field. Console has very practical features, such as copying queries as cURL requests, and vice versa:

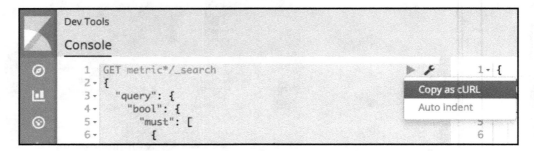

Copy as cURL

We'll use Console throughout this book, particularly for testing the different search, aggregation, and graph APIs.

Plugins

As opposed to core components, plugins are added to Kibana through a separate installation process, such as that we used for the X-Packs plugin. We'll go through them in this section.

DevTools/Profiler

Profiler allows a user to benchmark a given Elasticsearch query by breaking down the query by its features:

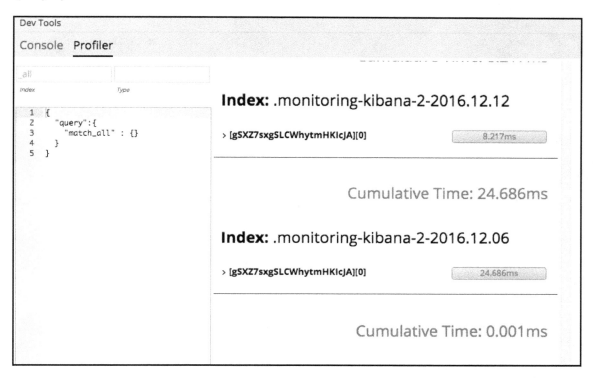

Profiler UI

The preceding screenshot shows the query to bench on the left and the result of the benchmark per indices on the right.

Monitoring

The monitoring plugin comes with X-Packs and allows the user to follow Elasticsearch and Kibana execution insights such as application health and resource consumption from a high-level point of view with top-level metrics, but also up to a given instance level:

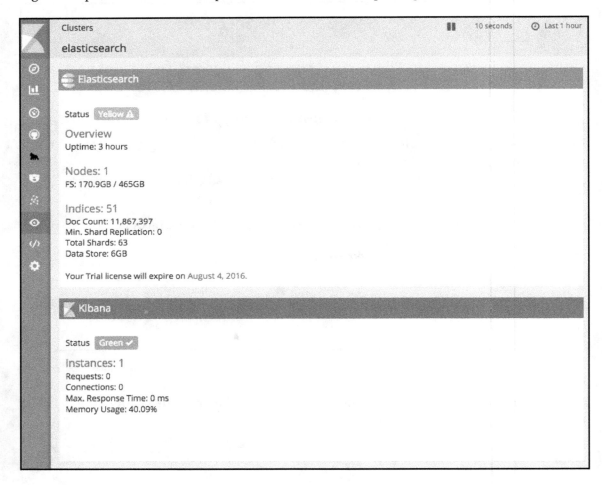

Monitoring landing page

The preceding landing page gives an overview of both Elasticsearch and Kibana health, which Kibana is new to the monitoring plugin. If you click on one or the other, you are brought to a detailed view of the related application:

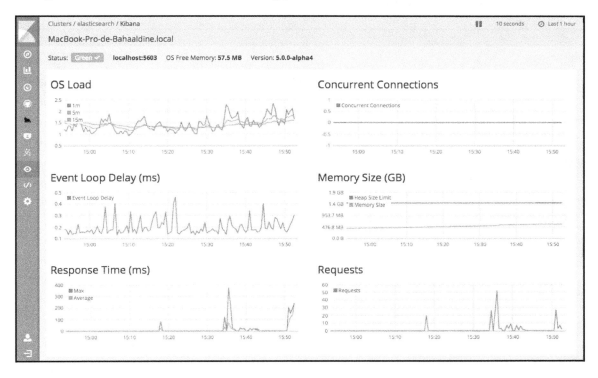

Kibana monitoring view

You can see some of the metrics that allow Kibana monitoring, such as the number of concurrent connections, which can be critical to follow when a problem occurs in an IT organization and everybody rushes to Kibana to diagnose the issue true story.

Graph

Graph is a plugin that also comes with X-Packs, and brings a way to visualize the data in the form of connections between documents; in other words, graphs:

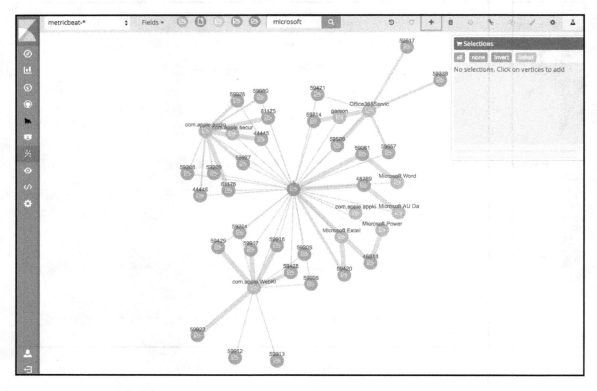

Graph visualization

The preceding example shows how you can leverage the MetricBeat data to reveal connections between process names and related PIDs.

In this book, we will use a more concrete use case to build recommendations on top of indexed data.

Summary

So far, we have looked at an example of the theory behind data-driven architecture in which Elasticsearch and Kibana play a key role: first at the storage layer, and second for the visualization section.

We also installed and set up Elasticstack, and walked through the different core and plugin components.

In the following chapters, we'll start implementing real-life use cases, starting with the logging use case, using accidentology data to try to understand the patterns of accidents that happen in Paris.

Business Analytics with Kibana 5.0

At this point, you should have the Elastic Stack installed and be able to start creating dashboards and visualizations. We will focus on the logging analytics use case in this chapter and dig into two examples: the Paris accidentology, which gives insights into traffic accidents in Paris; and server logging analytics, which gives insights into traffic over an Apache server.

The main topics we are going to see in this chapter are:

- How to import data in Elasticsearch with Logstash
- Building a Kibana dashboard from end to end
- Analyzing business data in Kibana

As a quick introduction to this chapter, I would like to devote few lines to the following question: What is a log?

A log is an event that contains a timestamp and a description of the event itself. It is appended to a journal or log file sequentially, and in which all lines of logs are ordered based on the timestamp. As an example, here is an Apache server log:

```
83.149.9.216 - - [28/May/2014:16:13:42 -0500] "GET /presentations/logstash-
monitorama-2013/images/kibana-search.png HTTP/1.1" 200 203023
"http://semicomplete.com/presentations/logstash-monitorama-2013/"
"Mozilla/5.0 (Macintosh; Intel Mac OS X 10_9_1) AppleWebKit/537.36 (KHTML,
like Gecko) Chrome/32.0.1700.77 Safari/537.36"
```

We can guess the meaning of certain information, such as an IP address (83.149.9.216), a timestamp (28/May/2014:16:13:42 -0500), an HTTP verb (GET), and the queried resource (/presentations/logstash-monitorama-2013/images/kibana-search.png). All this information is essential for different purposes, such as analyzing the traffic on your server, detecting suspicious behavior, or leveraging the data in order to enhance user experience on your website.

Before visualization applications came in as the de facto solution for analyzing logs, IT operations teams generally made massive GREP commands on this data in order to extract the gist of it. But this is not welcomed any more in environments where data is growing to reach a scale where is not humanly feasible to cope only with GREPs.

Kibana provides the ability to simplify log management, first through the visualization of the obvious, but also by discovering magic moments, in other words, unexpected data.

Business use case – Paris accidentology

You might wonder why I took Paris accidentology to illustrate the logging analytics use case. Well, I want to break into pieces the unfair reputation that sometimes sticks in people's minds when it comes to visualization with Kibana. Kibana is a visualization application; it's not only meant to be used by IT operations teams to monitor their application's health.

The name of the use case you are dealing with is just an abstraction that defines the use profile over your data. You can do logging analytics and actually deal with healthcare data, and do application monitoring with the same logs. It just depends on the nature and content of your data, also on the use profile of your visualization. If I put on my security hat, then I'll do security analytics on top of the ingested logs.

The Paris accidentology use case will help us to go through most of the visualizations and features that Kibana offers to implement logging analytics.

Data modeling – entity-centric documents

Like every product, the Elastic Stack comes with best practices for data modeling. Kibana renders the data that comes as a result of aggregation in Elasticsearch. Elasticsearch does aggregations on data in the same index. The index contains documents which contain fields. As a consequence, the more consisten documents are, the more scope you will have for aggregating data. By consistency in documents I mean as many fields as possible to describe an event, or in other words, an entity. This is what we call an entity-centric document.

In the case of our example, here is how the raw data is structured, hopefully:

```
20/04/2012 16:05,20/04/2012,16:05,75,111,"172, RUE DE LA
ROQUETTE",,1_75111_10314,,"172, RUE DE LA ROQUETTE, 75011 Paris",RUE
MERLIN,Motor Scooter,RESPONSIBLE,Car,RUN
AWAY,,,Cond,Injured,RESPONSIBLE,,,,,,,,,,,"172, RUE DE LA ROQUETTE, 75011
Paris",48.8591106,2.3862735,spring,2,afternoon
```

It's a comma-separated log line that describes an accident that occurred in Paris. It contains the timestamp of the accident, location information, a description of vehicles involved, and a description of people involved. If we transform this line into a proper JSON document, which is what Elasticsearch expects, here is what it looks like:

```
{
    "Address": "172, RUE DE LA ROQUETTE",
    "Zip code": null,
    "Dept": "75",
    "Person 2 Tag": null,
    "Segment": null,
  "Corner": "1_75111_10314",
    "Person 1 Category": "Cond",
    "involvedCount": "2",
    "Person 4 Cat": null,
    "season": "spring",
    "periodOfDay": "afternoon",
    "Person 3 Tag": null,
    "timestamp": "20/04/2012 16:05",
    "Com": "111",
    "Person 2 Category": null,
    "Person Tag": "RESPONSIBLE",
    "Vehicle 2 Description": "Car",
    "Hour": "16:05",
    "Vehicle 3 Description": null,
    "Person 3 Cat": null,
    "Address2": "RUE MERLIN",
    "Address1": "172, RUE DE LA ROQUETTE, 75011 Paris",
    "Person 4 Tag": null,
  "Date": "20/04/2012",
```

```
        "Vehicle 2": "RUN AWAY",
        "Vehicle 3": null,
        "Vehicle 1": "RESPONSIBLE",
        "Vehicle 1 description": "Motor Scooter",
        "fullAddress": "172, RUE DE LA ROQUETTE, 75011 Paris",
        "Person 2 Status": null,
        "location": {
          "lon": "2.3862735",
          "lat": "48.8591106"
        },
        "Person 4 Status": null,
        "Person 1 Status": "Injured",
        "Person 3 Status": null
}
```

The preceding commands are easier to read, and this is how we want to have it in Elasticsearch in order to have different possibilities in terms of aggregations. This will let us get certain information from the data, such as: what the most dangerous are streets in Paris, and how we can enhance the bicycling experience there. To import the CSV logs, we will use Logstash.

Importing data

Logstash is a server-side transformation component of the Elastic stack and will be used here to collect, transform, and send data to Elasticsearch.

Using Logstash

If we use Logstash, we need to build a configuration file and set the configuration of the different tiers: the file input, the filters, and the output. As this book is about using Kibana 5, I've prepare the configuration file that you will find in the Github repository so you won't have to learn all different Logstash configurations to get started.

I will describe each part of the configuration file, starting with the input.

Configuring the input – file

The input I'll use here is `file input`
(`https://www.elastic.co/guide/en/logstash/5.0/plugins-inputs-file.html`). This
input essentially ingests the data line by line from a file on a local filesystem:

```
input {
  file {
    path => "/path/to/accidents/files/directory/accident*"
    type => "accident"
    start_position => "beginning"
  }
}
```

The configuration starts by specifying a path to the file to ingest. You can see here that I'm
using a wildcard in case I have multiple source files that have the same name pattern.

I'm also setting a type, `accident`, which will be used as the document type in Elasticsearch.
The last `start_position` parameter is here to ask Logstash to start reading the file from
the beginning.

Setting the filters

Once you have your input in place, use the `filter` branch of the `Logstash`
`configuration` file to prepare the data before indexing it into Elasticsearch.

Here are the filters I'll use:

```
filter {
  csv {
    separator => ","
    columns => ["timestamp","Date","Hour","Dept","Com","Address","Zip
code","Corner","Segment","Address1","Address2","Vehicle 1
description","Vehicle 1","Vehicle 2 Description","Vehicle 2","Vehicle 3
Description","Vehicle 3","Person 1 Category","Person 1 Status","Person
Tag","Person 2 Category","Person 2 Status","Person 2 Tag","Person 3
Cat","Person 3 Status","Person 3 Tag","Person 4 Cat","Person 4
Status","Person 4
Tag","fullAddress","latitude","longitude","season","involvedCount","periodO
fDay"]
  }
  if ([Corner] == "Corner") {
    drop { }
  }
  date {
    match => [ "timestamp", "dd/MM/YYYY HH:mm" ]
    target => "@timestamp"
```

```
        locale => "fr"
        timezone => "Europe/Paris"
    }
    mutate {
        convert => [ "latitude", "float" ]
        convert => [ "longitude","float" ]
        rename => [ "longitude", "[location][lon]", "latitude",
"[location][lat]" ]
    }
}
```

The first filter is a `csv` filter that parses the event as comma-separated values. The column names specified here will be used as field names in the Elasticsearch JSON document. In the case of the first line of the source file, which represents the heads themselves, we don't want to retain them, so I'm using a small tick here to drop the file in the value of the column. `Corner` is actually `Corner` (the header name).

Then I'm playing with the date filter to format the date to the expected pattern and set the locale and the timezone.

Finally, the source file contains a longitude and a latitude field that I want to use to create a `geopoint` (`https://www.elastic.co/guide/en/elasticsearch/reference/master/geo-point.html`) field to render the accidents on a map.

Configuring the output – Elasticsearch

The last part is the output used to index data in Elasticsearch; the configuration is pretty straightforward:

```
output {
  elasticsearch {
    action => "index"
    hosts => "localhost:9200"
    index => "accidents-%{+YYYY}"
    user => "elastic"
    password => "changeme"
    template => "/path_to_template/template.json"
    template_overwrite => true
  }
}
```

It consists of putting in the correct settings so we can connect to Elasticsearch. The other part is setting the correct template path. A `template` is a file that describes the mapping used by an index (`https://www.elastic.co/guide/en/elasticsearch/reference/master/mapping.html`). The index will contain types that can be configured as well, for example, to set the field format. We are asking Logstash to use a template rather than letting Elasticsearch create a default template. This is because we want to make sure that the data will be correctly formatted for visualization in Kibana. For example, most of the text data, such as the `Address`, needs to be indexed as text but should have a keyword type field that will be used for aggregations in Kibana.

At this point, you are now able to run Logstash and ingest the data. Go into the Chapter 3 sources folder; you will find a `paris_accidentology` folder. Go into the `conf/logstash` directory and run the following:

```
MacBook-Pro-de-Bahaaldine:logstash bahaaldine$ ls
csv_to_es.conf   template.json
```

You should have the two preceding files, the `Logstash configuration` file and the index template.

You can run the following command to ingest the data:

```
MacBook-Pro-de-Bahaaldine:logstash bahaaldine$
/elastic/logstash-5.0.0/bin/logstash -f csv_to_es.conf
```

At the end of the ingestion, go to the **Console** section of Kibana and run the following command:

```
GET accident*/_count
```

You should have ingested about **13,628** documents. Now you are ready to visualize your data:

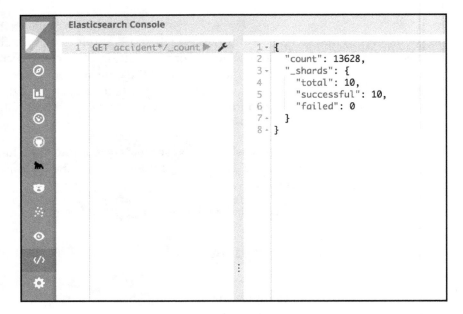

Counting documents in accident indices

Building the dashboard

Before starting to create a dashboard, it is worth understanding what happens under the hood when you create a visualization in Kibana at the query level. And we will see what happens in terms of queries when you combine visualizations in a dashboard as well.

Understanding the mechanics of a Kibana visualization with a line chart – the accident timeline

We will use the example of a line chart that represents the number of accidents which occurred over time. Hopefully, the creation process is the same across visualization types. We will describe this creation in detail, but will only focus on the differences for the next ones. To start the process, go to the **Visualization** section and choose to create a line chart:

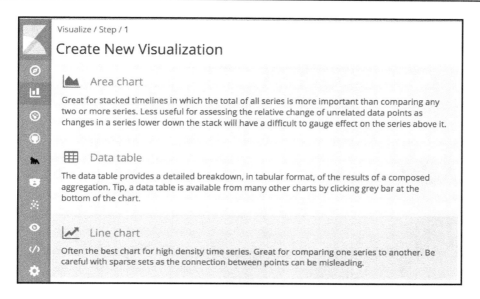

Creating a line chart

Choose the index pattern you want to work with; in this case, we're choosing `accident*`:

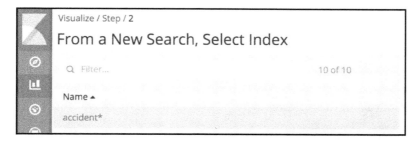

Choose the accident* index pattern

You will be brought to the line visualization setting section, which looks like the following screenshot:

Line chart options

There are two sections in the options:

- The metrics you want to use for the y axis. You can choose from a bunch of options, such as **Count**, **Average**, **Standard deviation**, and so on.
- The buckets options: you want to use the bucket value to draw an x axis, you want to **Split Lines**, or squarely split the chart.

In our case, we would like to draw the accident count on the y axis and the time on the x axis. We will leave **Count** for the y axis, set a custom label, `Accidents count`, and choose the x axis for the bucket configuration:

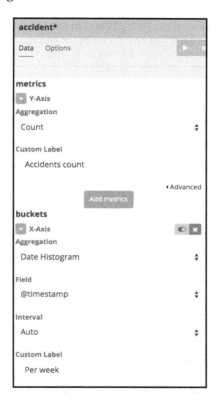

Line chart configuration

As you can see, to represent the time on the x axis I chose a **Date** histogram aggregation that will use the **@timestamp** field from each accident document. I left the interval configuration to Kibana, leaving the **Auto** option so that it will choose the optimal interval based on the number of buckets created by the aggregation. Essentially, if too many buckets are created you might not be able to show the data in a given time range. If you click on the Run button at the top of the options, you should get the following chart:

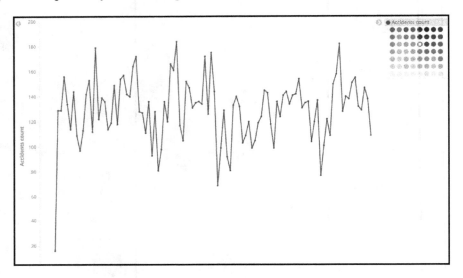

Accidents count line chart

There are some additional options for each chart type, if you click on **Options**:

Line chart options

For the line chart, I found the **Smooth Lines** option better than the default rendering option, which is a little bit too sharp:

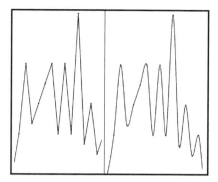

Sharp line versus Smooth line

On the left is the default sharp line, and on the right is the smooth line. Now that we have set the different options for our line chart, let's check what happens in terms of Elasticsearch queries under the hood. For this, you won't need to go very far; you just need to click on the little up arrow in the bottom-left corner of the chart:

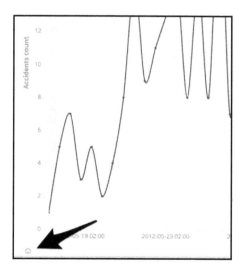

Visualization details view

The following table will be displayed:

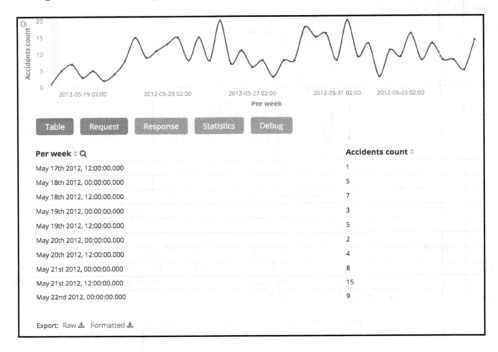

Visualization details

The details view comprises the following:

- A **Table** tab, which shows the data rendered on the chart as a table. Here, we have the timestamp and the accident count.
- A **Request** and a **Response** tab, which show the actual request sent to, and the response received from, Elasticsearch. We will come back to this.
- A **Statistics** tab, which shows the visualization statistics in terms of latency, for example.
- A **Debug** tab, to see the document that represents the visualization in Elasticsearch.

Going back to the request, here is what the line chart has generated:

```
{
  "size": 0,
  "query": {
    "bool": {
      "must": [
        {
          "query_string": {
            "analyze_wildcard": true,
            "query": "*"
          }
        },
        {
          "range": {
            "@timestamp": {
              "gte": 1337279849612,
              "lte": 1339020555494,
              "format": "epoch_millis"
            }
          }
        }
      ],
      "must_not": []
    }
  },
  "aggs": {
    "2": {
      "date_histogram": {
        "field": "@timestamp",
        "interval": "12h",
        "time_zone": "Europe/Berlin",
        "min_doc_count": 1
      }
    }
  }
}
```

The `query_string` part is used by the full text search bar if a query has been submitted, as the following screenshot shows:

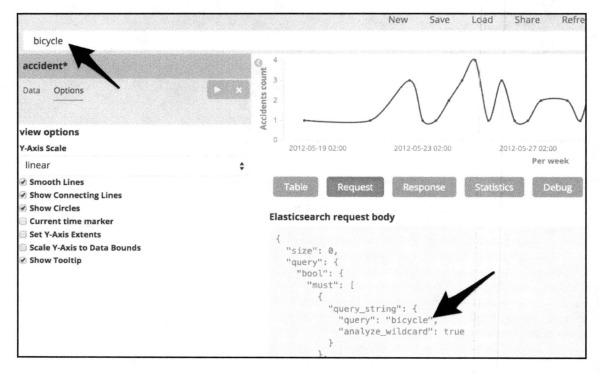

Using the full text search bar

The date range selects a time window in which the data will be rendered. The aggregation part uses the date histogram to create the count bucket over the specified interval. In our example, the data is counted into 12-hour buckets. The response contains the total documents per bucket. Here is an extract: you can get the complete response by clicking on the **Response** tab:

```
"aggregations": {
  "2": {
    "buckets": [
      {
        "key_as_string": "2012-05-17T12:00:00.000+02:00",
        "key": 1337248800000,
        "doc_count": 1
      },
      {
        "key_as_string": "2012-05-18T00:00:00.000+02:00",
```

```
    "key": 1337292000000,
    "doc_count": 5
},
{
    "key_as_string": "2012-05-18T12:00:00.000+02:00",
    "key": 1337335200000,
    "doc_count": 7
},
{
    "key_as_string": "2012-05-19T00:00:00.000+02:00",
    "key": 1337378400000,
    "doc_count": 3
},
```

We can see that for every 12 hours in our data a bucket is created and contains the doc_count, which in our example represents the number of accidents.

So, as you can see, all the aggregation magic is done at the Elasticsearch level, and Kibana takes the response and renders it. Now that you understand the mechanics under the hood, we can move on and create new charts for our accidentology dashboard. As in the preceding example, I will only focus on the differences rather than repeating the creation process, which is very similar across visualization types.

Bar chart – top accident streets

With the bar chart visualization type, we want to show the streets where most accidents happen. Start by going through the visualization creation process, and then select the **Vertical bar chart** type.

Then we will simply configure the buckets to display a term aggregation by selected x axis, and then picking the aggregation term from the combo box:

Bar chart settings

In the preceding screenshot, you can see that I've chosen to work with the non analyzed **Address.keyword**, which is needed to work with aggregation. Otherwise, if you try to make a term aggregation on an analyzed field, all terms contained in a field will be aggregated separately.

I also chose to set the size to 10 to get the top-10 most dangerous streets, in descending order. Finally, here is what you should get:

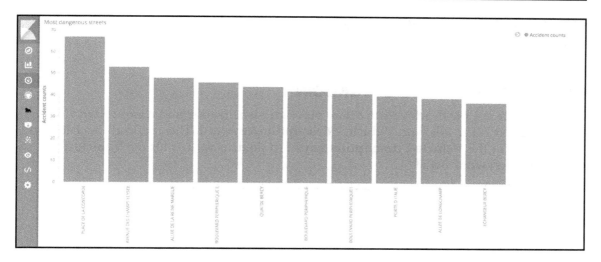

Top accident streets

You can go further and add another**bucket** by clicking on the **Add sub-bucket** button in the buckets section. This will allow you to add another level of aggregation, for example, creating a term aggregation on the **Vehicle 1 description.keyword** field. You will be able to see the most dangerous streets, each broken down by vehicle type:

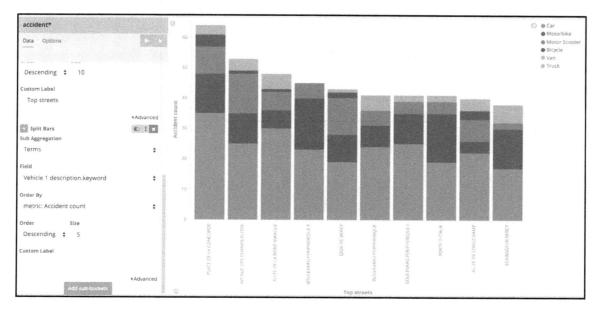

Top-10 dangerous streets with vehicles broken down

We will actually use this multi-level aggregation in order to show which vehicle types are involved in an accident.

Pie chart – vehicle breakdown

Our next chart is a pie chart. Create a new pie chart visualization and choose a term aggregation for the *x* axis with **Vehicle 1 description.keyword**. Then add sub-bucket term aggregation for the **Vehicle 2 description.keyword** field, as well as for the **Vehicle 3 description.keyword** field:

Multi-level aggregation in a pie chart

This is what you should get:

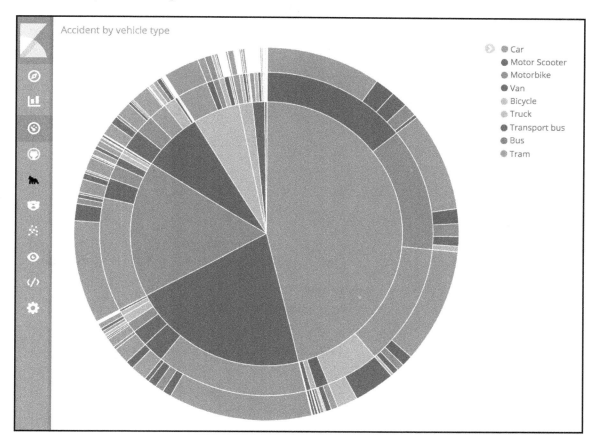

Involved vehicle breakdowns

This will allow a user to analyze based on the first vehicle type, and the second and third types that are involved, as the following example shows:

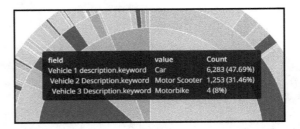

Vehicle involved in a car accident

Area chart – victim status

The following chart is an area chart that will break down the status of the person involved in a car accident. As with the previous chart, create an area chart with the following info:

- A **Date histogram** on the **@timestamp** field
- A sub-bucket that splits the area with a term aggregation in the **Person 1 status.keyword** field:

Area chart of accidents over time broken down by person status

So if you render the chart, you will get a stacked area chart, as the following screenshot shows:

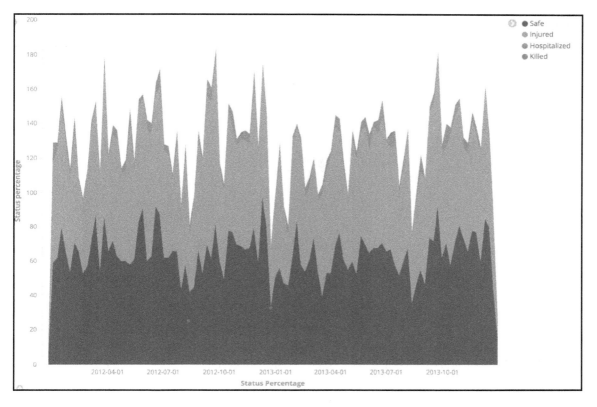

Stacked area chart

The preceding screenshot figure is, to me, not ideal to read a proportion, because it leaves an unused blank space at the top of the chart. We have a better setting in the Options tab, which lets us use percentages in place of the default stacked options, and this completely changes the visualization experience, as shown in the following screenshot:

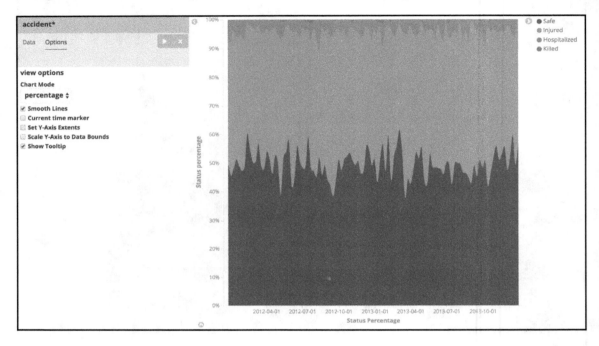

People's statuses after an accident

With percentages, the user is able to understand the victim status at a glance, and see, for example, that very few people are killed in accidents.

Tile map – accident data over a map

Our last chart will be a tile map on which we want to display the density of accidents in Paris. For that, just create a tile map, click on the geo coordinates, and you should have the location field automatically selected for the **Geohash** aggregation, as it's the only geopoint field in our document:

Tile map configuration

If you render the visualization, you should get the following as you zoom in on Paris:

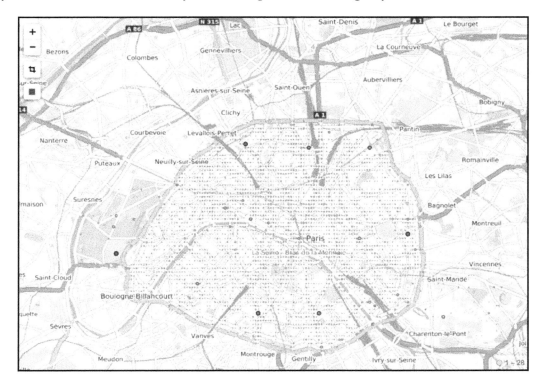

Accident map

Again, it is not ideal to visualize a proportion on a map, so if we go to the options tab we can switch from the default Scale circle markers to **Heatmap**. The **Heatmap** will show concentration of accidents on the map. You need to play with the settings in order to get an acceptable rendering. Here are the settings I've used:

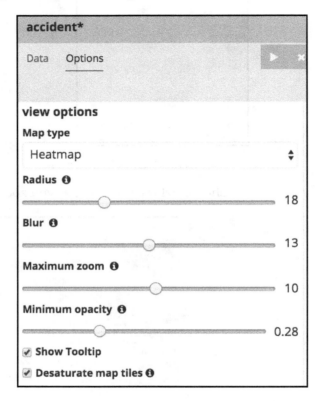

Heat map configuration

Radius is the size of the dots. The Blur setting decreases or increases the saturation of the heat. **Maximum zoom** depends on the zoom level of the map; as you zoom in, the saturation decreases above the **Maximum zoom** setting. **Minimum opacity** sets the saturation up to the **Maximum zoom**. Here is how the map renders with the heatmap enabled:

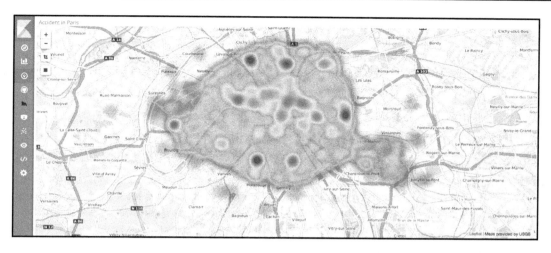

Accidents heatmap

At this point, we finally have all the visualizations to create our dashboard. To do so, go in the dashboard section and click on the **new** button in the top bar menu. From there, you can add visualizations by clicking on the **add** button. You can dispose of and scale visualizations as you want. Here is how I've done it:

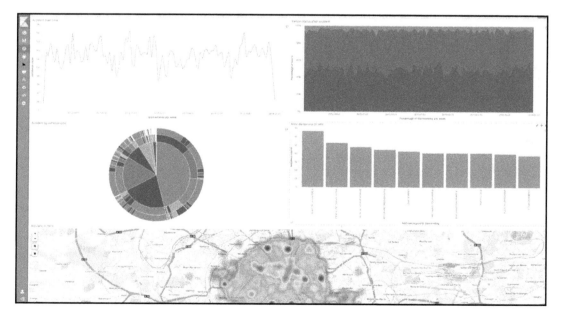

Paris accidentology dashboard

Asking questions of your data

Now that we have our dashboard ready, we can start to analyze our data, filter it, make some correlations, and discover patterns that we didn't expect or didn't think about. We can ask questions of our data.

How to enhance the bicycle experience in Paris?

Even if bicycles have been democratized in the streets of Paris for decade, and specifically with the Velib' network (https://en.wikipedia.org/wiki/V%C3%A9lib%27), the bicycling experience in Paris is known to be dangerous. With our dashboard, let's try to enhance the bicycling experience in Paris. To start, we can use our pie chart dashboard. Click on the **Bicycle** term in the legend and the magnifying glass with the plus icon:

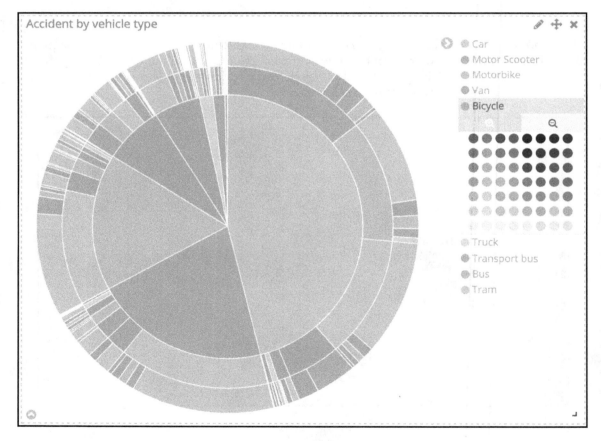

Filtering the dashboard by Bicyle

This will set a global filter for the whole dashboard and refresh the data:

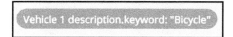

Bicycle filter

If we check the area chart, we can see that most people involved in a bicycle accident are injured. Surprisingly, not many are hospitalized or killed, which is unexpected given Paris' reputation for bicycling:

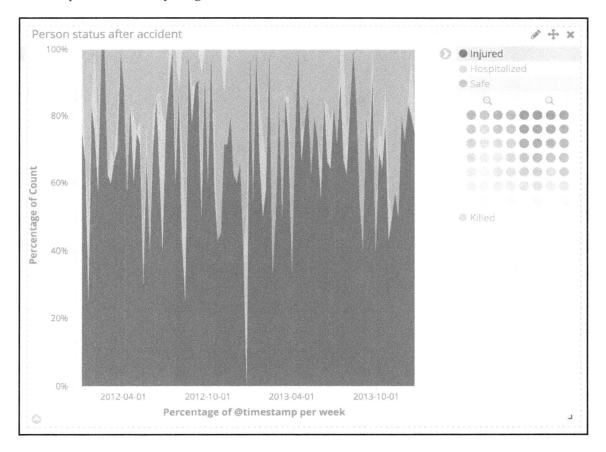

Bicycle accident victim status

Now, if we check the map, we can see that most of the accidents occur in a vertical axis that crosses Paris from North to South:

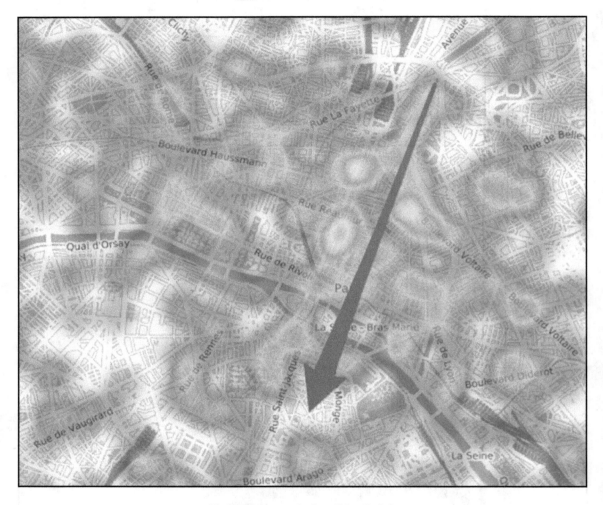

Bicycle accident concentration shows a line crossing Paris

This axis is known to have a lot of traffic as it crosses the city center. If you check the pie chart, you will also notice that, beside cars, a variety of vehicles are involved in the accidents:

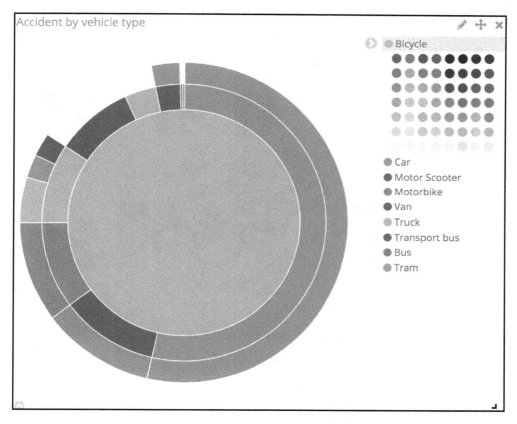

Vehicles involved in bicycle accidents

We can express the hypothesis that bicycles share the road with other vehicles on this axis (at the time of this study). As a consequence, there might be an opportunity to enhance the user experience there by adding bicycle lanes. It's not easy to build bicycle lanes in Paris because of the lack of space, which is why we do have logical lanes, which essentially are drawn on the road. They narrow down the road even more, as the following picture shows (source: `https://en.wikipedia.org/wiki/Bicycle-sharing_system`):

Bicycle lane

This is the first conclusion we can take from the mental journey we took on Kibana. Now we can also leverage other features, such as the full text search feature. If we take the heatmap again, we can see that, globally, the bicycle accident concentration is not very different from the background data:

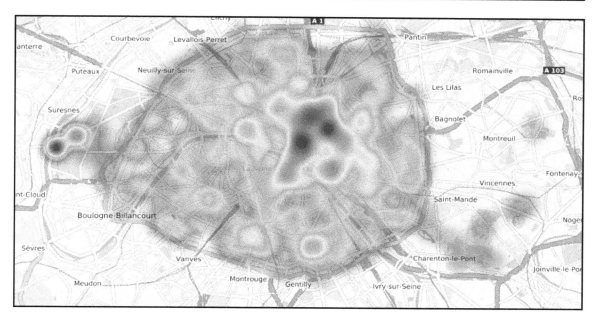

High level heatmap of bicycle accidents

Try to analyze the morning commute by issuing the **morning** keyword in the full text search bar:

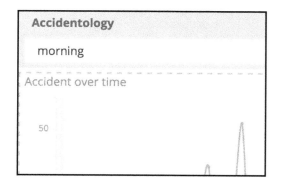

Filtering by period of day: morning

Here is what we get on the heatmap:

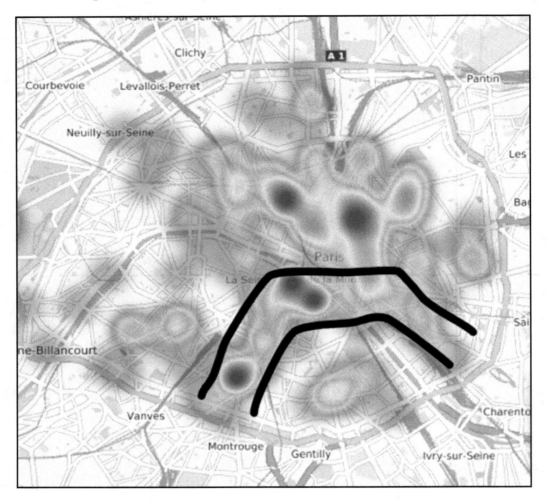

Bicycle accidents concentration on morning commute

If you know Paris, you should not be surprised to see a high concentration of accidents in the north of Paris but, as the preceding screenshot shows, there is a region surrounded by a black line that is worth more attention.

In this region of Paris, there are a lot of schools and universities, so we can see that there is another opportunity here to enhance the experience of students bicycling to school by drawing or building dedicated lanes.

What are the most dangerous streets in Paris, and why?

It could also be very interesting to identify the most dangerous streets in Paris and understand why this is the case.

To do so, we can use a bar chart, which essentially gives us the **Most dangerous streets** based on the number of accidents:

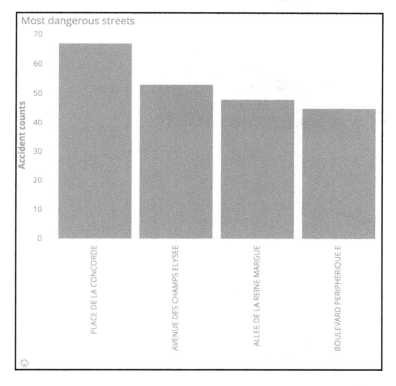

Top-4 most dangerous streets in Paris

Again, if you know Paris, you won't be surprised to find **Place de la Concorde** as well as **Avenue des Champs Elysees** in the results, which are a very large roundabout and a crowded street in Paris, respectively.

The third one is, let's say, more intriguing: **Allée de la Reine Marguerite**, is almost not even in Paris; it's on the western border:

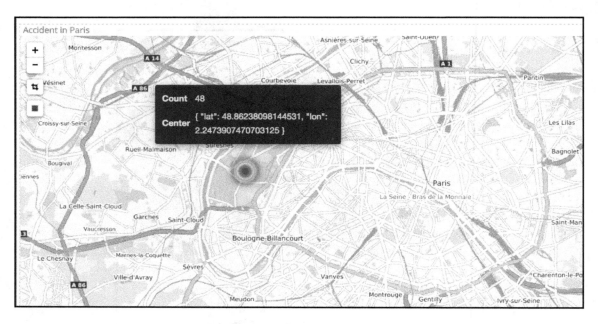

Accidents near Allée de la Reine Marguerite

From the pie chart, you will see that most accidents are caused by cars, but also unexpectedly by vans; furthermore, additional vehicles involved are bicycles, motorbikes, and motor scooters:

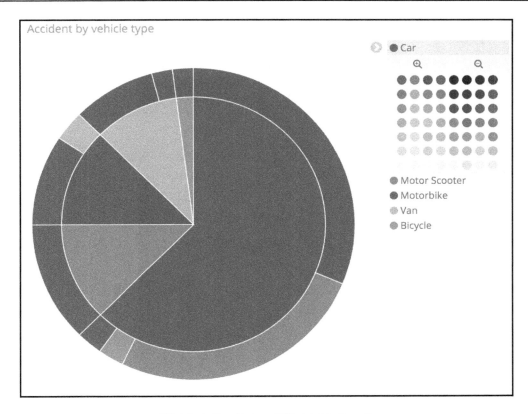

Vehicles involved in accidents near AllÃ©e de la Reine Marguerite

It's well known that, in Paris, accidents with two-wheelers happen when drivers don't check their blind spots. So, that would mean that cars and vans are unexpectedly pulling over in this area. Why?

Prostitution.

Indeed, parts of West and East Paris are infamous for prostitution. It's a hypothesis, but vehicles could be pulling over to meet the prostitutes.

Summary

Here ends our business analysis chapter on Paris accidentology. You should have a good vision of how to build a pipeline in Logstash to import data from a CSV file or any other sources. Also, we have seen how to compose a dashboard with different types of visualization, with the aim of applying business analytics questions to our data.

The next chapter addresses a more technical topic, namely Apache server logging analytics. The methodology is the same; we'll just use a different approach to import data and obviously ask different questions.

4

Logging Analytics with Kibana 5.0

The previous chapter showed how to use the Elastic stack for a business (logging) use case, which confirms that Elastic is not only a solution made for technical use cases, but rather a data platform that you can shape depending on your needs.

In the logging use case field, one of the most implemented within the technical domain is the web server logging use case. This chapter is a continuation of the previous one in the sense that we are dealing with logs, but addresses the problem from a different angle.

The goal here is first to understand the web logs use case, then to start importing both data in Elasticsearch, and dashboards in Kibana. We will go through the different visualizations available as part of the dashboard to see what key performance indicators can be extracted from the logs.

Finally, we'll ask our dashboard a question and deduce some more high-level considerations from the data, such as security or bandwidth insights.

Technical use case – Apache server logs

Apache and NGINX are the most used web servers in the world; there are billions of requests served by those servers out there, to internal networks as much as to external users. Most of the time, they are one of the first logic layers touched in a transaction, so from there, one can get a very precise view of what is going on in term of service usage.

In this chapter, we'll focus on the Apache server, and leverage the logs that the server generates during runtime to visualize user activity. The logs we are going to use were generated by a website (`www.logstash.net`) Apache web server. They were put together by Peter Kim and Christian Dahlqvist, two of my solutions architect colleagues at Elastic (`http s://github.com/elastic/elk-index-size-tests`).

As mentioned in the introduction, this data can be approached and analyzed from different angles, and we will try to proceed to a security and a bandwidth analysis.

The first aims to detect suspicious behavior in the data, such as users trying to access pages that do not exist on the website using an admin word in the URL; this behavior is very common. It's not rare to see websites such as *WordPress* blogs that expose an administration page through the `/wp-admin` URI. People who look for security leaks know this and will try to take advantage of it. So, using our data, we can aggregate by HTTP code (here, `404`) and see what the most visited unknown pages are.

The second aims to measure how the traffic behaves on a given website. The traffic pattern depends on the website; a regional website might not be visited overnight, and a worldwide website might have constant traffic, but if you break down the traffic per country, you should get something similar to the first case. Measuring the bandwidth is then crucial to ensuring an optimal experience for your users, so it could be helpful to see that there are regular peaks of bandwidth consumption coming from users in a given country.

Before diving into the security and bandwidth analysis section, let's look at how to import data in Elasticsearch, and the different visualizations you will have to import available as part of the dashboard.

Importing data in Console

The data we are dealing with here is not very different in terms of structure than in the previous chapters. They are still events that contain a timestamp, so essentially, time-based data. The sample index we have contains 300,000 events from 2015.

The way we'll import the data is slightly different than in the previous chapter, where we used Logstash to index the data from a source file. Here, we'll use the snapshot API provided by Elasticsearch. It allows us to restore a previously created index backup. We'll then restore a snapshot of the data provided as part of the book's resources.

Here is the link to the Elasticsearch snapshot-restore API (`https://www.elastic.co/guide/en/elasticsearch/reference/master/modules-snapshots.html`), in which you need more in-depth information.

The following are the steps to restore our data:

- Set the path to a snapshot repository in the Elasticsearch configuration file
- Register a snapshot repository in Elasticsearch
- List the snapshot and check whether it appears in the list, to see whether our configuration is correct
- Restore our snapshot
- Check whether the index has been restored properly

We first need to configure Elasticsearch to register a new path to a repository of the snapshot. To do so, you will need to edit the `elasticsearch.yml`, located here:

ELASTICSEARCH_HOME/conf/elasticsearch.yml

Here, `ELASTICSEARCH_HOME` represents the path to your Elasticsearch installation folder.

Add the following settings at the end of the file:

path.repo: ["/PATH_TO_CHAPTER_3_SOURCE/basic_logstash_repository"]

`Basic_logstash_repository` contains the data in the form of a snapshot. You can now restart Elasticsearch to apply the changes into account.

Now open Kibana and go to the **Console** section. Console is a web-based Elasticsearch query editor that allows you to play with the Elasticsearch API. One of the benefits of Console is that it brings auto-completion to what the user types, which helps a lot when you don't know everything about the Elasticsearch API.

In our case, we'll use the snapshot/restore API to build our index; here are the steps to follow:

1. First you need to register the newly added repository using the following API call:

```
PUT /_snapshot/basic_logstash_repository
{
  "type": "fs",
  "settings": {
  "location":
    "/Users/bahaaldine/Dropbox/Packt/sources/chapter3/
      basic_logstash_repository",
```

```
        "compress": true
    }
}
```

2. Once registered, try to get the list of snapshots available to check the registration worked properly:

   GET _snapshot/basic_logstash_repository/_all

   You should get the description of our snapshot:

```
{
  "snapshots": [
    {
      "snapshot": "snapshot_201608031111",
      "uuid": "_na_",
      "version_id": 2030499,
      "version": "2.3.4",
      "indices": [
      "basic-logstash-2015"
      ],
      "state": "SUCCESS",
      "start_time": "2016-08-03T09:12:03.718Z",
      "start_time_in_millis": 1470215523718,
      "end_time": "2016-08-03T09:12:49.813Z",
      "end_time_in_millis": 1470215569813,
      "duration_in_millis": 46095,
      "failures": [],
      "shards": {
      "total": 1,
      "failed": 0,
      "successful": 1
      }
    }
  ]
}
```

3. Now, launch the restore process with the following call:

   POST
   /_snapshot/basic_logstash_repository/snapshot_201608031111/_restore

   You can request the status of the restore process with the following call:

   GET
   /_snapshot/basic_logstash_repository/snapshot_201608031111/_status

In our case, the data volume is so small that the restore should only take a second, so you might get the success message directly, and no intermediary state:

```
{
  "snapshots": [
    {
      "snapshot": "snapshot_201608031111",
      "repository": "basic_logstash_repository",
      "uuid": "_na_",
      "state": "SUCCESS",
      "shards_stats": {
        "initializing": 0,
        "started": 0,
        "finalizing": 0,
        "done": 1,
        "failed": 0,
        "total": 1
      },
      "stats": {
        "number_of_files": 70,
        "processed_files": 70,
        "total_size_in_bytes": 188818114,
        "processed_size_in_bytes": 188818114,
        "start_time_in_millis": 1470215525519,
        "time_in_millis": 43625
      },
      "indices": {
        "basic-logstash-2015": {
          "shards_stats": {
            "initializing": 0,
            "started": 0,
            "finalizing": 0,
            "done": 1,
            "failed": 0,
            "total": 1
          },
          "stats": {
            "number_of_files": 70,
            "processed_files": 70,
            "total_size_in_bytes": 188818114,
            "processed_size_in_bytes": 188818114,
            "start_time_in_millis": 1470215525519,
            "time_in_millis": 43625
          },
          "shards": {
            "0": {
              "stage": "DONE",
              "stats": {
```

```
                    "number_of_files": 70,
                    "processed_files": 70,
                    "total_size_in_bytes": 188818114,
                    "processed_size_in_bytes": 188818114,
                    "start_time_in_millis": 1470215525519,
                    "time_in_millis": 43625
                }
            }
        }
      }
    }
  }
 ]
}
```

At this point, you should be able to list the newly created index. Still in Console, issue the following command:

GET _cat/indices/basic*

This is what Console should look like at this stage:

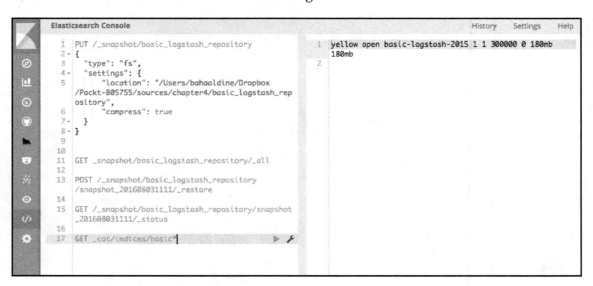

Restoring the data from Console

The response indicates that our index has been created and contains 300,000 documents.

There could be different approaches here to what index topology we should use: because the data has timestamps, we could, for example, create daily indices, or weekly indices. This is very common in a production environment, as the most recent data is often the most used. Thus, from an operations point of view, if the last seven days of logs are the most important ones and you have daily indices, it's very handy to set up routines that either archive or remove the old indices (older than seven days).

If we look at the content of our index, here is an example of a document extract:

```
"@timestamp": "2015-03-11T21:24:20.000Z",
"host": "Astaire.local",
"clientip": "186.231.123.210",
"ident": "-",
"auth": "-",
"timestamp": "11/Mar/2015:21:24:20 +0000",
"verb": "GET",
"request": "/presentations/logstash-scale11x/lib/js/head.min.js",
"httpversion": "1.1",
"response": 200,
"bytes": 3170,
"referrer": ""http://semicomplete.com/presentations/logstash-scale11x/"",
"agent": ""Mozilla/5.0 (Macintosh; Intel Mac OS X 10_9_0)
AppleWebKit/537.36 (KHTML, like Gecko) Chrome/32.0.1700.102
Safari/537.36"",
"geoip": {
  "ip": "186.231.123.210",
  "country_code2": "BR",
  "country_code3": "BRA",
  "country_name": "Brazil",
  "continent_code": "SA",
  "latitude": -10,
  "longitude": -55,
  "location": [
    -55,
    -10
  ]
},
"useragent": {
  "name": "Chrome",
  "os": "Mac OS X 10.9.0",
  "os_name": "Mac OS X",
  "os_major": "10",
  "os_minor": "9",
  "device": "Other",
  "major": "32",
```

```
    "minor": "0",
    "patch": "1700"
}
```

The document describes a given user connection to the website and is composed of HTTP metadata, such as the version, the return code, the verb, the user agent with the description of the OS and device used, and even localization information.

Analyzing each document would not make it possible to understand website-user behavior; this is where Kibana comes into play, by allowing us to create visualizations that will aggregate data and reveal insights.

We can now import the dashboard.

Importing the dashboard

Unlike in the previous chapter, we won't create the visualization here, but rather use the Import feature of Kibana, which lets you import Kibana objects such as searches, visualizations, and dashboards that already exist. All these objects are actually JSON objects indexed in a specific index called, by default, .kibana.

Go into the management section of Kibana and click on **Saved Objects**. From there, you can click on the **Import** button and choose the JSON file provided in the book's resources. First import the Apache-logs-visualizations.json file, and then the Apache-logs-dashboard.json file. The first contains all the visualizations, and the second contains the dashboard that uses the visualizations. The following visualizations should be present:

Management / Kibana

Index Patterns   **Saved Objects**   Reporting   Advanced Settings

Edit Saved Objects   [⬇ Export Everything]   [⬆ Import]

From here you can delete saved objects, such as saved searches. You can also edit the raw data of saved objects. Typically objects are only modified via their associated application, which is probably what you should use instead of this screen. Each tab is limited to 100 results. You can use the filter to find objects not in the default list.

Basic

Dashboards (0)   Searches (0)   Visualizations (13)

☐ Select All   [🗑 Delete]   [⬇ Export]

☐ Basic Elastic Summary

☐ Basic ELK - Summary

☐ Basic Logstash - Summary

☐ Basic Logstash - US vs CA

☐ Basic Logstash 404 vs 404 mavg(5)

☐ BasicLogstash - Bandwidth by Country

☐ BasicLogstash - HeatMap

☐ BasicLogstash - Map

☐ BasicLogstash - Metrics

☐ BasicLogstash - Requests by Agent

☐ BasicLogstash - Response Codes over Time

☐ BasicLogstash - Significant Countries by Response Code

☐ BasicLogstash - Top Requested Resources

Imported Visualizations

You will have all the **BasicLogstash** visualizations.

Let's review the imported dashboard. Go to the **Dashboard** section and try to open the **Elastic Stack-Apache Logs** dashboard. You should get the following:

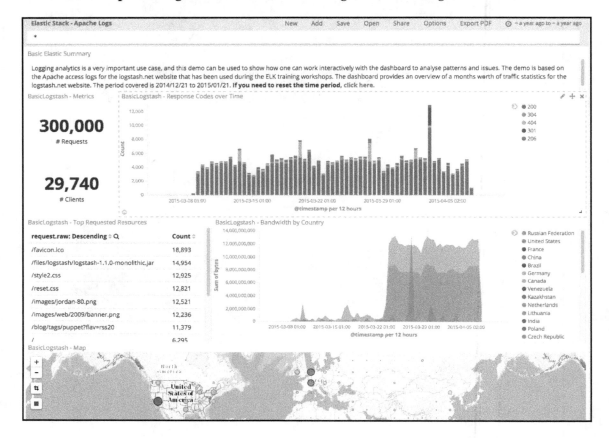

Apache log dashboard

At this stage, we are now ready to browse the visualizations one by one and explain what they mean.

Understanding the dashboard

We'll now go through each visualization and look at the key performance indicators and features they provide:

Markdown – notes in dashboard

The following is the screenshot of the basic Elastic summary:

Basic Elastic Summary

Logging analytics is a very important use case, and this demo can be used to show how one can work interactively with the dashboard to analyse patterns and issues. The demo is based on the Apache access logs for the logstash.net website. The dashboard provides an overview of a months worth of traffic statistics for the logstash.net website. The period covered is 2014/12/21 to 2015/01/21. **If you need to reset the time period,** click here.

Markdown visualization

The markdown visualization can be used to add comments to your dashboard, such as in our example, to explain what the dashboard is about. You can also leverage the support of URLs to create a menu, so the user is able to switch from one state of the dashboard to another.

Kibana stores its state in the URL, which is how you can share a specific state of a dashboard just by sharing the link.

Metrics – logs overview

The following metrics visualization gives a summary about the data presented in the dashboard:

BasicLogstash - Metrics

300,000
Requests

29,740
Clients

Apache logs metrics

It's always useful to have some metrics displayed in your dashboard, so, for example, you can keep track of the number of documents affected by your filtering while you play with the dashboard.

Bar chart – response code over time

Bar charts are great for visualizing one or more dimensions of your data over time. In this example, we are showing a breakdown of response code over time. Thus, you can see the volume of requests on `www.logstash.net` and whether there is a change compared to what you think is the expected behavior. The following shows some **404** spikes that might need a closer look:

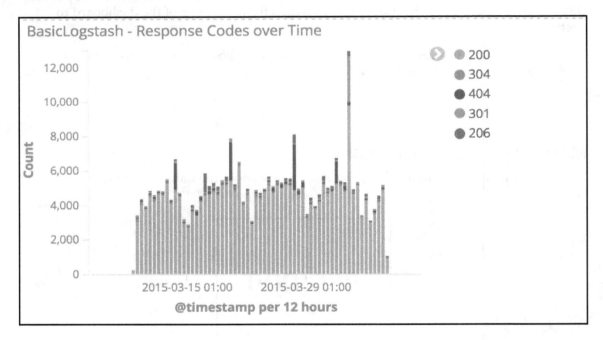

Response codes over time

Area chart – bandwidth by country

Area charts are useful for displaying accumulative data over time. Here, we are using the country location field to build this area chart, to give us insights on which countries are connecting to our website:

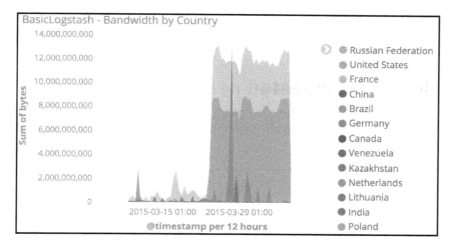

Bandwidth by country

We will look at how we can use this information in the context of bandwidth analysis later in the chapter.

Data table – requests by agent

Data table charts can be used to display tabular field information and values. Here, we are displaying a count of the user-agent field, which allows us to understand the types of clients connecting:

BasicLogstash - Requests by Agent	
agent.raw: Descending $\updownarrow$ Q	Count $\updownarrow$
"Chef Client/10.18.2 (ruby-1.8.7-p302; ohai-6.14.0; x86_64-linux; +http://opscode.com)"	14,072
"-"	11,092
"Mozilla/5.0 (Windows NT 6.1; WOW64; rv:27.0) Gecko/20100101 Firefox/27.0"	10,151
"Mozilla/5.0 (X11; Ubuntu; Linux x86_64; rv:27.0) Gecko/20100101 Firefox/27.0"	8,773
"UniversalFeedParser/4.2-pre-314-svn +http://feedparser.org/"	8,529

Requests by agent

We will see that in the context of security analytics, this can be a very useful piece of information to identify a security anomaly.

Data table – top requested resources

When a host connects to your website, you might to know what to what is the resource is browsing for different reason such as click-stream analysis, or security wise; this is what the following data table gives you:

BasicLogstash - Top Requested Resources	
/images/jordan-80.png	12,521
/images/web/2009/banner.png	12,236
/blog/tags/puppet?flav=rss20	11,379
/	6,295
/presentations/fpm-scale12x.pdf	5,327
/?flav=rss20	5,103

Export: Raw ⬇ Formatted ⬇

Top requested resources

This is also an asset that we'll use in the security analysis.

Pie chart – significant countries by response

The response bar chart already represents two dimensions, where a dimension here is a field contained in our document. We could eventually split by country, but the analysis experience would be a little bit complicated. Instead, we could use a pie chart to show the country breakdown based on the response code, as shown here:

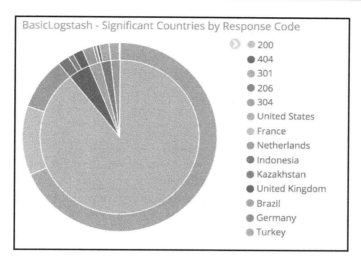

Significant countries by response code

Tile map – hits per country

The data contains host geo-point coordinates. Here, we are using this information to graph client connections onto a tile map of the world. Again, from a pure analytics point of view, the fact that countries are mentioned across visualizations wouldn't be enough if they were not drawn on the map as follows:

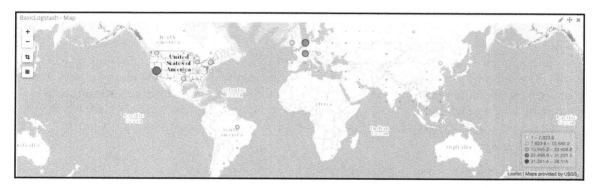

Hits per countries

Furthermore, the map visualization will allow you to draw polygons to narrow down your analysis.

Asking the data a question

Once the dashboard is created, the idea is to ask it questions by interacting with one or more visualizations. This will narrow down the analysis and isolate the particular patterns that are the answers to our questions.

Bandwidth analysis

You may have noticed in the bandwidth by country that the level is low between August 2015 and the end of March 2015 and then suddenly, for an unknown reason, it increases significantly. We see a marked increase in the data downloaded, represented by the arrow on the graph:

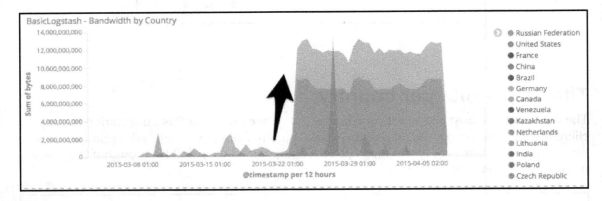

Bandwidth increase

We can zoom into this time region of the chart, which will also zoom in all other charts to within the same time range. If you read the requests by the agent data table, you will notice that the first user agent is a Chef agent. Chef is used by operations teams to automate processes such as installation, for example. Since the data we have comes from `www.logstash.net`, we can deduce that a Chef agent is connecting to our website for installation purposes.

If you click on the Chef row in the data table, this will apply a dashboard filter based on the value of the field you selected. This allows you to drill into your data, narrowing down your analysis, and we can easily conclude that this process consumes the majority of the bandwidth:

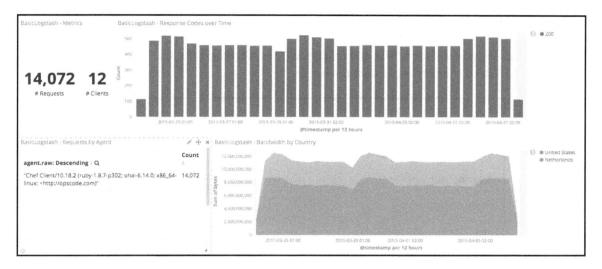

Chef bandwidth utilization

With a few clicks, we have been able to point out a bandwidth utilization issue and are now able to take the proper measures to throttle the connection of such agents to our website. From there, we will switch to a different angle of analysis: security.

Security analysis

In this section, we'll try to look for a security anomaly, which is defined as an unexpected behavior in the data; in other words, data points that are different from normal behavior observed in the data, based on the facts that our dashboard shows us.

If you reset the dashboard by reopening it, you will notice in the bar chart that a significant amount of **404** responses happen sporadically in the background of the hits:

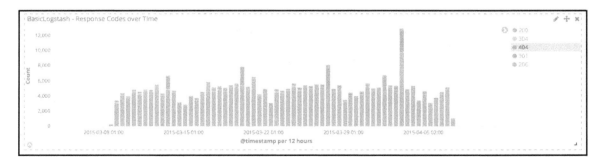

404 responses

Click on the **404** code in the legend to filter the dashboard and refresh the other visualizations and data table. You will notice in the user-agent data table that an agent called – is the source of a lot of the **404** responses. So, let's filter the analysis by clicking on it. Now have a look to the top requested resources:

BasicLogstash - Top Requested Resources	
request.raw: Descending ⇕ Q	**Count** ⇕
/wp/wp-admin/	79
/blog/wp-admin/	76
/wordpress/wp-admin/	73
/wp-admin/	71

Top requested resources by user agent "-"

There is a very unusual, possibly suspicious activity, such as an attempt to attack our website. Basically, the **wp-admin** URI is the resource to access the WordPress blog admin console. However, in our case, the website is not a WordPress blog.

New WordPress users may not have the knowledge to either change or disable the admin console on their site, and might also use the default user/password. So, my guess here is that the user agent tried to connect to the **wp-admin** resource and issue the default credentials to take total control of our website.

Summary

In this chapter, we have looked at how to use Kibana 5.0 in the context of technical logging use cases by diving into the analysis of Apache server logs. We have learned how to leverage visualizations for different purposes, such as bandwidth or security analysis. In the next chapter, we'll get into the domain of metrics analysis by first using Beats, the Elastic Stack data shipper.

5
Metric Analytics with Metricbeat and Kibana 5.0

In the two previous chapters, we have seen how to use Kibana in order to visualize log data in the context of a business and a technical use case. We will now focus on metric analytics, which is fundamentally different in terms of data structure.

So, before starting this chapter, I would like to devote a few lines to the following question:

What is a metric?

A **metric** is an event that contains a timestamp and usually one or more numeric values. It is appended to a metric file sequentially, where all metric lines are ordered based on the timestamp. As an example, here are a few system metrics:

```
02:30:00 AM    all    2.58    0.00    0.70    1.12    0.05    95.55
02:40:00 AM    all    2.56    0.00    0.69    1.05    0.04    95.66
02:50:00 AM    all    2.64    0.00    0.65    1.15    0.05    95.50
```

Unlike logs, metrics are sent periodically, for example, every 10 minutes (as the preceding example illustrates) whereas logs are usually appended to the log file when something happens.

Metrics are often used in the context of software or hardware health monitoring, such as resource utilization monitoring, database execution metric monitoring, and so on.

Since version 5.0, Elastic has had, at all layers of the solutions, new features to enhance the user experience of metric management and analytics. Metricbeat is one of the new features in 5.0. It allows the user ship metrics data, whether from the machine or from applications, to Elasticsearch, and comes with out-of-the-box dashboards for Kibana. Kibana also integrates Timelion with its core, a plugin designed to manipulae numeric data, such as metrics.

In this chapter, we'll start by working with Metricbeat and then use one of the X-Pack components, alerting, to introduce Timelion, before exploring it in more detail in the next chapter.

Technical use case – system monitoring with Metricbeat

Metricbeat is way more than just a system metric shipper. It has an extensible module architecture that comes with out-of-the-box-modules, as illustrated in the following diagram:

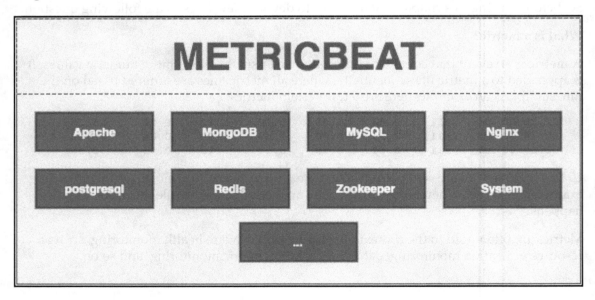

Metricbeat architecture

As shown in the preceding diagram, Metricbeat is capable of shipping metrics from web servers (**Apache**, **Nginx**), databases (**MongoDB**, **MySQL**, **postgresql**), and even **Redis** or **Zookeeper**. Furthermore, Elastic provides online documentation for developers who want to create their own Metricbeat, so one can easily extend the out-of-the-box features.

In this book, we'll use the system module, which comes as the default configuration of Metricbeat. You will be able to monitor your computer or laptop and visualize the data in Kibana 5.0. This is just an example of what you will be able to do with Metricbeat. If you think on a larger scale, you can imagine distributing Metricbeat shippers all over a datacenter, using a centralized Kibana instance to monitor all the nodes.

Getting started with Metricbeat

In this part we'll go through the installation of Metricbeat, and start shipping data to Elasticsearch.

Metricbeat installation

Installing Metricbeat is as easy as decompressing a TAR file. First, download it at `https://www.elastic.co/downloads/beats/metricbeat`:

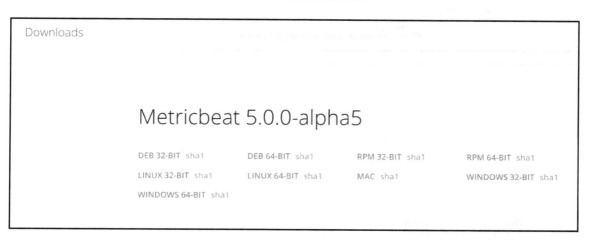

In my case, I'm downloading 5.0.0-alpha5 (the current version at the time of writing) and the Mac archive, and uncompressing the TAR file:

```
tar -zxvf metricbeat-5.0.0-darwin-x86_64.tar.gz
```

You should get the following directory structure:

```
MacBook-Pro-de-Bahaaldine:metricbeat-5.0.0 bahaaldine$ pwd
/elastic/metricbeat-5.0.0
MacBook-Pro-de-Bahaaldine:metricbeat-5.0.0 bahaaldine$ ls
total 23528
scripts
metricbeat.yml
metricbeat.template.json
metricbeat.template-es2x.json
metricbeat.full.yml
metricbeat
```

At this point, Metricbeat is installed and needs to be configured to fit your environment settings.

Configuring and running Metricbeat

Metricbeat's configuration is stored in the Metricbeat.yml file. It's composed of the following sections:

- **Modules**: This is the part where one specifies the modules that need to be used
- **General**: Here are the shipper configurations, such as its name, for example
- **Outputs**: Here, the user can specify whether he wants to send the data to Logstash and Elasticsearch
- Metricbeat logging configuration

We'll leave all the configurations defaults in force and only focus on the output part. What we want is to send our metrics data to our Elasticsearch instance, so go into the *Outputs* section of the configuration and change the settings there to fit your configuration:

```
#======================= Outputs ==================================
# Configure what outputs to use when sending the data collected by
  the beat.
# Multiple outputs may be used.
#------------------------- Elasticsearch output --------------------
    -------------
output.elasticsearch:
  # Array of hosts to connect to.
  hosts: ["localhost:9200"]
  # Optional protocol and basic auth credentials.
  #protocol: "https"
  #username: "elastic"
  #password: "changeme"
```

In our case, as we are using the default security settings in 5.0 with X-Pack installed, we need to pass a user and a password. Let's not use the default, and instead create a new user dedicated to Metricbeat. To do so, open Kibana and go into the **Management** section:

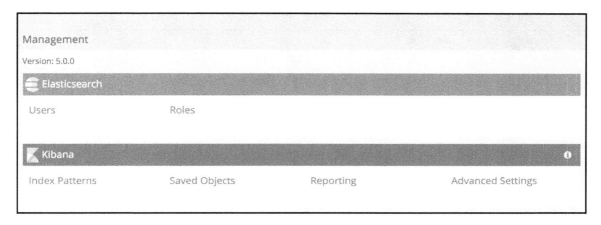

Kibana management panel

Once there, click the **Roles** link. You will be brought to the following page:

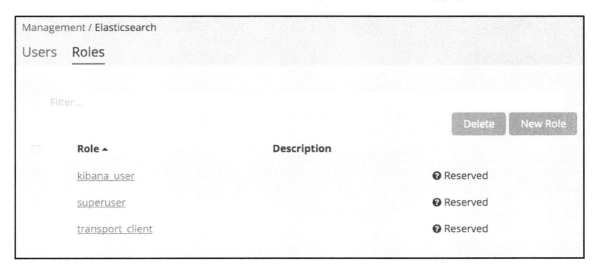

Click on the **New Role** button to create a new role. The role configuration panel lets you create a role with a very fine granularity from cluster to field-level security. In our example, we'll take a shortcut and create a role that has the privileges to create indices and store our metrics:

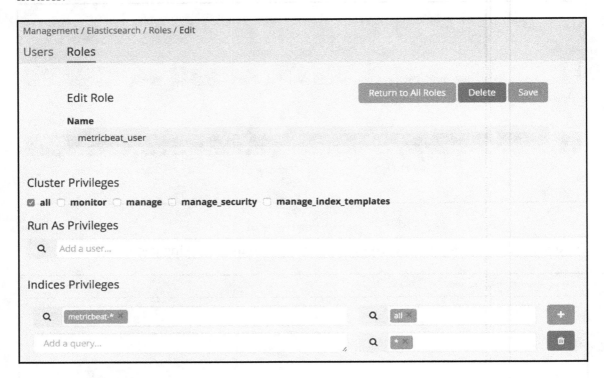

Create the metricbeat_user role

As you can see, the role will be able to create indices that follow the metricbeat-* pattern, which is the default index pattern that Metricbeat uses. Also, we gave all privileges on these indices.

Save the role and go into the user section to create a new **metricbeat_user** by clicking on the **New User** button:

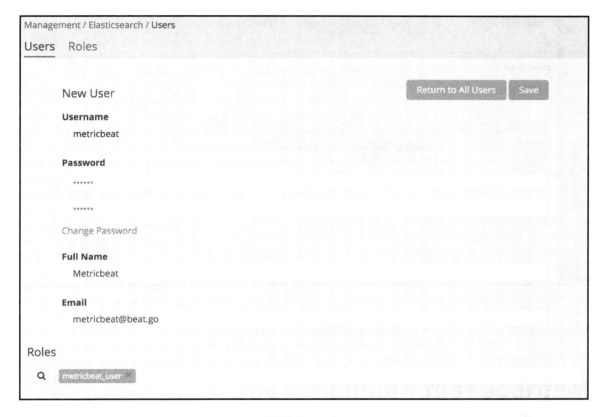

Metricbeat user creation

You can now adapt metricbeat.yml and add the credentials you've just created:

```
# Optional protocol and basic auth credentials.
#protocol: "https"
username: "metricbeat"
password: "secret"
```

We are ready to run Metricbeat and to ship data to Elasticsearch. Run the following command in the Metricbeat installation directory:

```
mac:metricbeat-5.0.0 bahaaldine$ ./metricbeat
```

If you go back into Kibana and go into the **Discover** tab and select the **metricbeat*** index pattern, you should see data flowing in Elasticsearch:

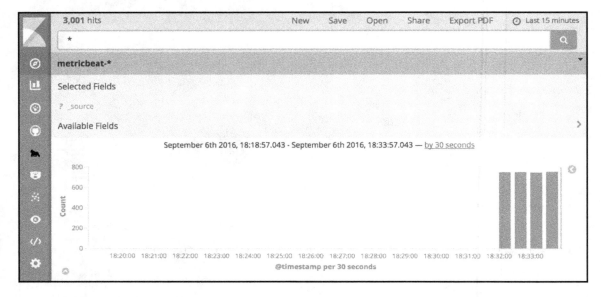

Metricbeat data coming in Elasticsearch

We are now ready to import Metricbeat Kibana dashboards.

Metricbeat in Kibana

In this section, we'll focus on the different visualization the Metricbeat installation ships out-of-the-box in Kibana.

Importing the dashboard

Before importing the dashboard, let's have a look at the actual metric data that Metricbeat ships. As I have Chrome opened while typing this chapter, I'm going to filter the data by process name, here **chrome**:

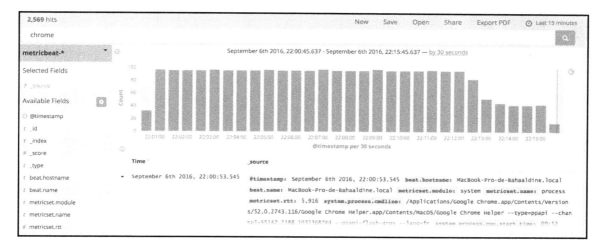

Discover tab filtered by process name

Here is an example of one of the documents I have:

```
{
  "_index": "metricbeat-2016.09.06",
  "_type": "metricsets",
  "_id": "AVcBFstEVDHwfzZYZHB8",
  "_score": 4.29527,
  "_source": {
    "@timestamp": "2016-09-06T20:00:53.545Z",
    "beat": {
      "hostname": "MacBook-Pro-de-Bahaaldine.local",
      "name": "MacBook-Pro-de-Bahaaldine.local"
    },
    "metricset": {
      "module": "system",
      "name": "process",
      "rtt": 5916
    },
    "system": {
      "process": {
        "cmdline": "/Applications/Google
          Chrome.app/Contents/Versions/52.0.2743.116/Google Chrome
          Helper.app/Contents/MacOS/Google Chrome Helper --type=ppapi -
          -channel=55142.2188.1032368744 --ppapi-flash-args --lang=fr",
        "cpu": {
          "start_time": "09:52",
          "total": {
            "pct": 0.0035
          }
```

```
        },
      "memory": {
        "rss": {
          "bytes": 67813376,
          "pct": 0.0039
        },
        "share": 0,
        "size": 3355303936
      },
      "name": "Google Chrome H",
      "pid": 76273,
      "ppid": 55142,
      "state": "running",
      "username": "bahaaldine"
      }
    },
    "type": "metricsets"
  },
  "fields": {
    "@timestamp": [
      1473192053545
    ]
  }
}
```

The preceding document breaks down the utilization of resources for the **chrome** process. We can see, for example, the of CPU and memory use, as well as the state of the process as a whole. Now how about visualizing the data in an actual dashboard? To do so, go into the `script` folder located in the Metricbeat installation directory:

```
MacBook-Pro-de-Bahaaldine:scripts bahaaldine$ pwd
/elastic/metricbeat-5.0.0/scripts
MacBook-Pro-de-Bahaaldine:kibana bahaaldine$ ls
import_dashboards.sh
```

`import_dashboards.sh` is the file we will use to import the dashboards in Kibana. Execute the file script as follows:

```
./import_dashboards.sh -h
```

This should print out the help, which, essentially will give you a list of arguments you can pass to the script. Here, we need to specify a username and a password as we are using the X-Pack security plugin, which secures our cluster:

```
./import_dashboards.sh -u elastic:changeme
```

You should normally get a bunch of logs stating that dashboards have been imported, as shown in the following example:

```
Import visualization Servers-overview:
{"_index":".kibana","_type":"visualization","_id":"Servers-
overview","_version":4,"forced_refresh":false,"_shards":
{"total":2,"successful":1,"failed":0},"created":false}
```

Now, at this point, you have metric data in Elasticsearch and dashboards created in Kibana, so you can now visualize the data.

Visualizing metrics

If you go back into the Kibana/dashboard section and try to open the **Metricbeat system overview** dashboard, you should get something similar to the following:

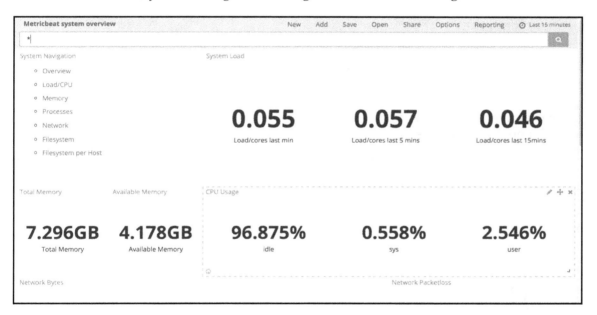

Metricbeat Kibana dashboard

You should see in your own dashboard the metric based on the processes that are running on your computer. In my case, I have a bunch of them for which I can visualize the CPU utilization and system load by clicking on the Load/CPU section:

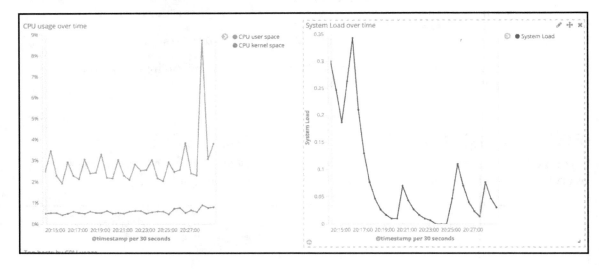

CPU utilization and system load

As an example, the important point here is to be sure that Metricbeat has a very low footprint on the overall system in terms of CPU or RAM, as shown here:

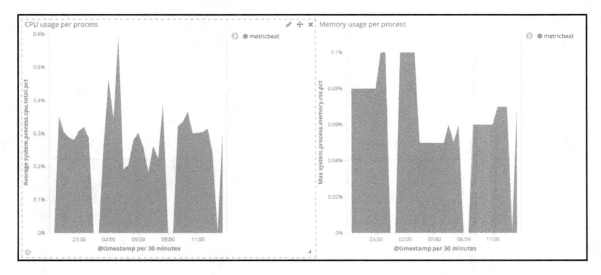

Metricbeat resource utilization

As we can see in the preceding diagram, Metricbeat only uses about **0.4%** of the CPU and less than **0.1%** of the memory on my Macbook Pro. On the other hand, if I want to get the most resource-consuming processes, I can check in the **Top processes** data table, which gives the following information:

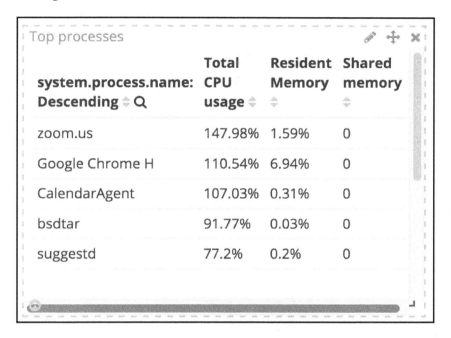

system.process.name: Descending ⇕ Q	Total CPU usage ⇕	Resident Memory ⇕	Shared memory ⇕
zoom.us	147.98%	1.59%	0
Google Chrome H	110.54%	6.94%	0
CalendarAgent	107.03%	0.31%	0
bsdtar	91.77%	0.03%	0
suggestd	77.2%	0.2%	0

Top processes

Besides **Chrome H**, which uses a lot of CPU, **zoom.us**, a conferencing application, seems to stress my laptop a lot.

Rather than using the Kibana standard visualization to manipulate our metrics, we'll use Timelion instead, and focus on this heavy CPU consumption use case.

Metricbeat in Timelion

Timelion is a fantastic visualization tool to manipulate time series data; here, we'll go through examples of usage based on Metricbeat data.

Analyzing the max CPU utilization over time

As explained earlier in this book, Timelion is the new Kibana core plugin that allows the user to manipulate numeric fields in terms of mathematical operations and visualize them graphically. In this section, we'll introduce Timelion using the previous example, where we analyzed the top processes.

Let's start by logging in to Kibana and clicking on the **Timelion** icon in the side bar:

Kibana menu side bar

The first thing you will notice is a welcome banner that will guide you through the fundamental Timelion features, as the user experience is very different from the usual Kibana dashboard:

Welcome to **timelion** the timeseries expression interface for

everything

Timelion. Timeline. Get it? Ok, enough with the puns. Timelion is the, clawing, gnashing, zebra killing, pluggable timeseries interface for *everything*. If your datastore can produce a timeseries, then you have all of the awesome power of Timelion at your disposal. Timelion lets you compare, combine and combobulate (not actually a word) datasets across multiple data sources, even entirely different technologies, all with the same easy-to-master expression syntax. While the beginning of this tutorial will focus on Elasticsearch, once you're rolling you'll discover you can use nearly everything you learn here with any datasource timelion supports.

Why start with elasticsearch? Well, you're using timelion, so we know you have Kibana, so you definitely have Elasticsearch. So the answer is: **Because its easy.** Timelion want everything to be easy. Ok, let's do this thing. If you're already familar with Timelion's syntax, Jump to the function reference, otherwise click the **Next** button in the lower right corner.

Don't show this again   Next

Timelion welcome banner

Besides what you will learn in this book, I recommend that you walk through the welcome tutorial.

What you will also notice is a workspace composed of an expression bar and one or more charts:

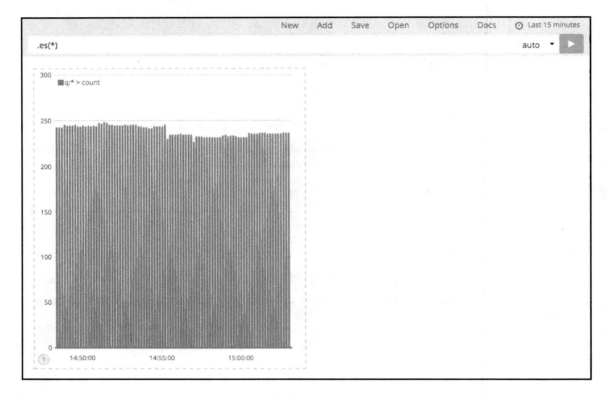

Timelion workspace

The top menu bar lets you do the following:

- Create a new workspace (**New**)
- Add a new chart to a workspace (**Add**)
- Save a workspace (**Save**)
- Open a workspace (**Open**)
- Access display options (**Options**)
- Access the documentation (**Docs**)
- Change the time range with the time picker

The expression bar allows you to create a Timelion expression that points to one or more data sources, not just Elasticsearch. That's one of the main differences with Kibana dashboards, where the only possible data source is Elasticsearch. Here, you can use Quandl, Worldbank, Graphite, and even develop your own data source.

A data source expression essentially issues a request to get a list of numeric data. In the case of Elasticsearch, the result is aggregation buckets; this isn't different from what you would find with Kibana dashboards.

Then, using mathematical expressions, Timelion lets you make calculations, approximations, and other extrapolations on the result set. So Timelion essentially delegates the heavy lifting to the underlying data source technologies, such as Elasticsearch, and applies metric transformation on the browser side.

This comes with the downside that the result set must not exceed a maximum of **2,000** metric buckets:

Max bucket error banner

This guarantees that the volume of data will not be too heavy for browser-based calculation. This is what the interval picker to the right of the expression bar lets you configure:

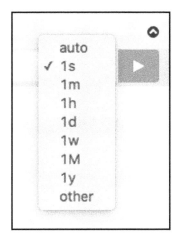

Timelion interval picker

By default, auto is selected and fulfills most use cases; we'll see an example of this use in this section. If we now check the expression bar, you should have the following default expression:

`.es(*)`

This expression points to our Elasticsearch cluster and counts all the documents within the period selected in the time picker. This is then rendered on the only chart you have so far, as expression a per chart. Now let's use this data source and point to the `metricbeat*` index pattern, using the following expression:

`.es(index=metricbeat*)`

The `index` argument allows you to point to a specific `index` pattern, which gives us the following diagram:

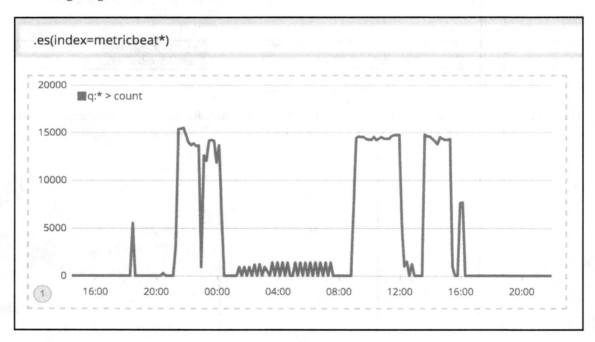

metricbeat* documents count

Now how about filtering the chart to only show documents for which the total CPU used is greater than 100%, like this:

```
.es(index=metricbeat*, q=system.process.cpu.total.pct:>1.0)
```

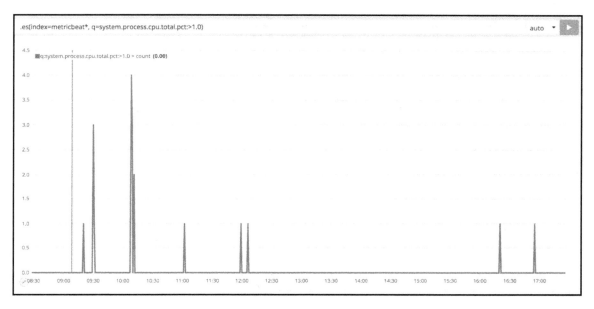

Process for which the CPU is over 100%

The q or query argument allows you to set a filter, and, in our example, get a view of the number of processes for which the CPU is over 100%. We can see that it sporadically appear over time.

We can have a different view on this use case by using the metric argument and showing the maximum CPU usage over time.

This time we'll add more complexity to the visualization as we will introduce a way to visualize CPU variation in line with a threshold, and by tagging with a cross all data points that have gone over the threshold.

So first, let's show the maximum CPU usage over time:

```
.es(index=metricbeat*,
metric=max:system.process.cpu.total.pct:>1.0).color(#2196F3).label("Max CPU
over time")
```

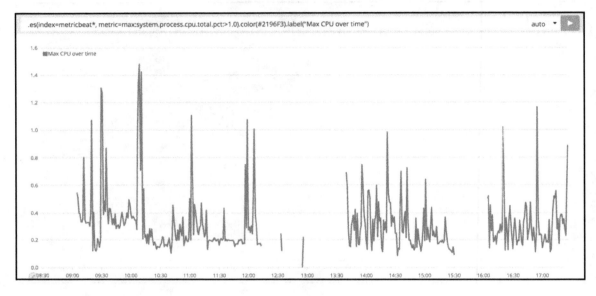

Maximum CPU usage over time

We used the `metric` argument with the max operation to calculate the max on the series list, and as you can see there are some holes in the chart (basically, for whatever, reason my laptop wasn't running, or was closed). Here, we can guess that I took a break for lunch and was maybe traveling around 3:30 pm.

Where we are missing data points, which happens in a lot of different use cases, due to network crashes, for example, we can use another function called **fit** that interpolates the data to connect the dots based on a given mode:

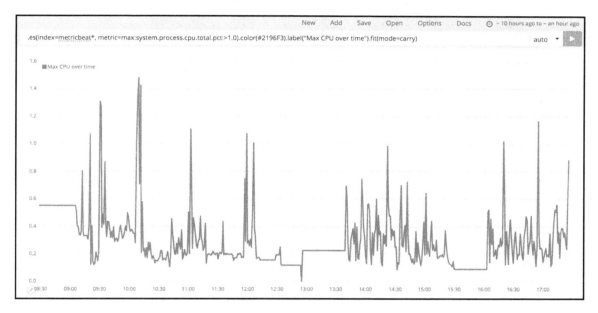

Fitting the missing part with the carry mode

I've intentionally used `carry` mode in the fit function as it gave the best results for the max operation in my case. Don't hesitate to try the others, knowing that some of them, such as scale, are not ideal for the max case. You can find the documentation for each mode directly in the code comments at
`https://github.com/elastic/timelion/tree/master/server/fit_functions.`

OK, the next step is to print two thresholds on the chart, in other words, a static line that represents a warning value and another one that represents a value above which serious action should be taken. Let's arbitrarily state that when CPU use exceeds 75%, this our warning value, and 100% is the critical threshold. Add this to the expression:

```
.static(0.75).color(#FF9800).label(Warning),
.static(1.0).color(#F44336).label(Error)
```

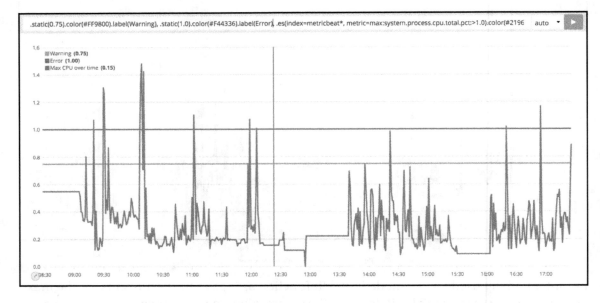

Chart with thresholds

The `color` and `label` expressions bring customization features to the chart, with each line having a specific color and legend label.

We can smooth the max CPU graph a little bit by adding the `movingaverage` function:

```
.es(index=metricbeat*,
metric=max:system.process.cpu.total.pct:>1.0).color(#2196F3).label("Max CPU
over time").fit(mode=carry).movingaverage(2)
```

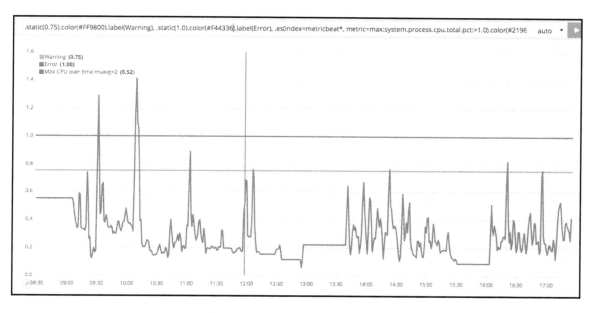

Smoothing the line with the moving average function

Now we can mark the data points that reach the threshold using the `points` function, and multiply everything by 100 to visualize percentage values:

```
(.static(0.75).color(#FF9800).label(Warning),
.static(1.0).color(#F44336).label(Error),
.es(index=metricbeat*,
metric=max:system.process.cpu.total.pct:>1.0).color(#2196F3).label("Max CPU
over time").fit(mode=carry).movingaverage(2), .es(index=metricbeat*,
metric=max:system.process.cpu.total.pct:>1.0).color(#2196F3).fit(mode=carry
).movingaverage(2).condition(lt, 0.75).condition(gt,
1.0).points(symbol=diamond, radius=4).color(#EF6C00).label("1st level
alert"),
.es(index=metricbeat*,
metric=max:system.process.cpu.total.pct:>1.0).color(#2196F3).fit(mode=carry
).movingaverage(2).condition(lt, 1.0).points(symbol=diamond,
radius=4).color(#FF1744).label("2nd level alert")).multiply(100)
```

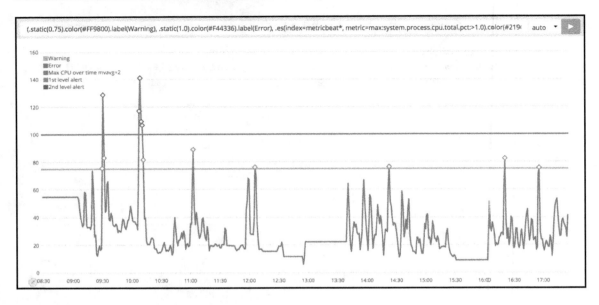

Tagged values

The preceding expression is less complex than we think; I'm just reusing the same expression I've used to draw the max CPU line to display the orange diamond (`.condition(lt, 0.75).condition(gt, 1.0)`) and the red diamond (`.condition(lt, 1.0)`).

Now we have a complete chart that display a smooth metric-based max CPU utilization line with real-time anomaly-tracking points. We can very simply see where the value goes above the threshold in the same chart. Let's save the chart into a Kibana panel by clicking the **Save** button and then **Save current expression as Kibana dashboard panel**:

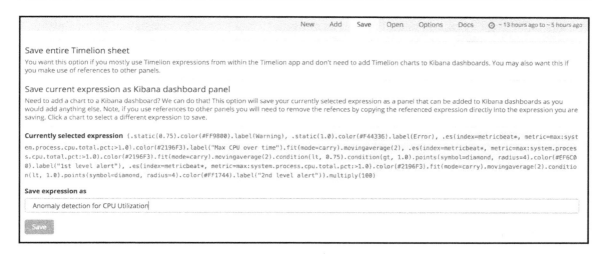

Then, go into the dashboard section and add it to the Metricbeat System Statistic dashboard by clicking the **Add** button. Here is how it should look:

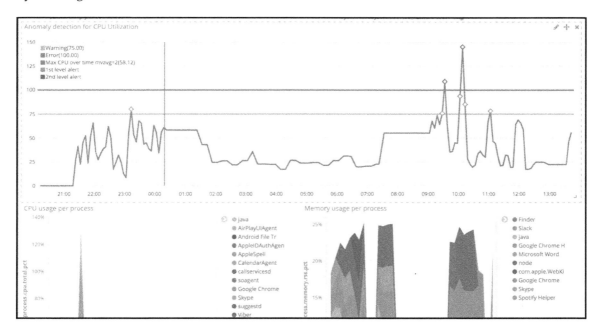

Kibana 5.0 brings a holistic visualization experience to the users by consistently combining visualization features.

In the next part, we'll enhance our visualization by adding alerting capabilities and visualizing when the alerts have actually been triggered.

Using X-Pack alerting

We first need to create an alert, which is, essentially, composed of the following features:

- A **trigger**: How often the alert should be triggered
- An **input**: The data the alert will use
- A **condition**: The rule that will execute the alert action
- An **action**: The channel where the alert result should be sent

If you need more information about alerting, I recommend you go through the online documentation found at
`https://www.elastic.co/guide/en/x-pack/current/xpack-alerting.html`.

In our case, we want to trigger an alert when the maximum system CPU consumption goes over 40%. This means we will work with the `system.process.cpu.total.pct`, which gives this value, and here is what our alert looks like:

```
{
  "trigger": {
    "schedule": {
      "interval": "10s"
    }
  },
  "input": {
    "search": {
      "request": {
        "indices": [
          "metricbeat*"
        ],
        "body": {
          "size": 0,
          "aggs": {
            "max_cpu": {
              "max": {
                "field": "system.process.cpu.total.pct"
              }
            }
          },
```

```
                "query": {
                  "bool": {
                    "must": [
                      {
                        "range": {
                        "@timestamp": {
                          "gte": "now-10s"
                        }
                      }}
                    ]
                  }
                }
              }
            }
          },
          "condition" : {
            "script" : {
              "lang": "painless",
              "inline" : "if (ctx.payload.aggregations.max_cpu.value > 0.40) {
return true; } return false;"
            }
          },
          "actions": {
            "log": {
              "transform": {},
              "logging": {
                "text": "Max CPU alert executed : {{ctx}}"
              }
            },
            "index_payload" : {
              "transform": {
                "script": {
                  "lang": "painless",
                  "inline": "Map result = new HashMap(); result['@timestamp'] =
ctx.trigger.triggered_time; result['cpu'] =
ctx.payload.aggregations.max_cpu.value; return result;"
                }
              },
              "index" : {
                  "index" : "cpu-anomaly-alerts",
                  "doc_type" : "alert"
              }
            }
          }
        }
      }
```

As you can see, the alert is triggered every 10 seconds; it executes the input request, which essentially aggregates the data, and calculates the maximum system value over the data Metricbeat has been sending for the last 10 seconds.

Then the condition verifies whether the value is above 0.4 (40%) and, if so, executes the alert actions:

- Logging a message that contains all the context data within the ctx variable. Here is an example of the output:

```
[2016-09-12 22:16:40,159][INFO ][xpack.watcher.actions.logging]
[Jaguar] Max CPU alert executed : {metadata=null,
watch_id=cpu_watch, payload={_shards={total=35, failed=0,
successful=35}, hits={hits=[], total=225, max_score=0.0},
took=2, timed_out=false, aggregations={max_cpu=
{value=0.7656000256538391}}}, id=cpu_watch_53-2016-09-
12T20:16:40.155Z, trigger={triggered_time=2016-09-
12T20:16:40.155Z, scheduled_time=2016-09-12T20:16:39.958Z},
vars={}, execution_time=2016-09-12T20:16:40.155Z}
```

- Indexing part of the alert output in cpu-anomaly-alerts, such as the time it has been triggered and also the maximum CPU value:

```
{
  "_index": "cpu-anomaly-alerts",
  "_type": "alert",
  "_id": "AVcgA-viVDHwfzZYssj_",
  "_score": 1,
  "_source": {
    "@timestamp": "2016-09-12T20:08:30.430Z",
    "cpu": 0.5546000003814697
  }
}
```

To use this alert, we need to go into the Kibana **Console** plugin and add it to the alerts index. There is a dedicated X-Pack API for this:

```
Elasticsearch Console

84 ▾ }
85
86
87
88    PUT _xpack/watcher/watch/cpu_watch        ▶  🔧
89 ▾ {
90 ▾    "trigger": {
91 ▾      "schedule": {
92          "interval": "10s"
93 ▴      }
94 ▴    },
95 ▾    "input": {
96 ▾      "search": {
97 ▾        "request": {
98 ▾          "indices": [
99              "metricbeat*"
100 ▴         ],
101 ▾         "body": {
102             "size": 0,
103 ▾           "aggs": {
104 ▾             "max_cpu": {
105 ▾               "max": {
106                   "field": "system.process.cpu.total.pct"
107 ▴               }
108 ▴             }
109 ▴           },
110 ▾           "query": {
111 ▾             "bool": {
112 ▾               "must": [
113 ▾                 {
114 ▾                   "range": {
115 ▾                     "@timestamp": {
116                         "gte": "now-10s"
```

Creating an alert in Kibana Console

After doing this, we are now ready to go back into Kibana Timelion and adapt our expression in order to draw our maximum CPU line and the data point where an alert has been triggered. Here is the expression I've used:

```
(
    .static(0.4).color(#FF9800).label(Warning),
        .es(index=metricbeat*, metric=max:system.process.cpu.total.pct)
     .color(#2196F3)
     .label("Max CPU over time")
     .fit(mode=carry).movingaverage(2),
    .es(index=cpu-anomaly-alerts)
     .condition(operator=lt,1)
     .points(symbol=cross)
     .color(#FF1744)
    .divide(
        .es(index=cpu-anomaly-alerts)
        .condition(operator=lt,1)
    )
    .multiply(
        .es(index=metricbeat*,
etric=max:system.process.cpu.total.pct)
        .fit(mode=carry)
        .movingaverage(2)
    )
).multiply(100)
```

The expression starts by creating a static line that represents our 40% threshold. Then I draw the moving average of the maximum system CPU used. Then I use the cpu-anomaly-alerts index, which holds all the alert outputs, to draw a cross whenever an alert is triggered.

Note that I'm using a condition that eliminates all points equal to zero from the visualization because Timelion will draw them, which could result in a chart that seems heavy and cluttered.

I divide this same dataset by itself so that I'll get a cross where each value is one, and multiply it by the same expression used for the maximum system CPU. So, to streamline all the values on the charts, I just need one *Y* axis, and the cross should overlap the CPU line. Finally, I multiply everything by 100 to visualize the percentage:

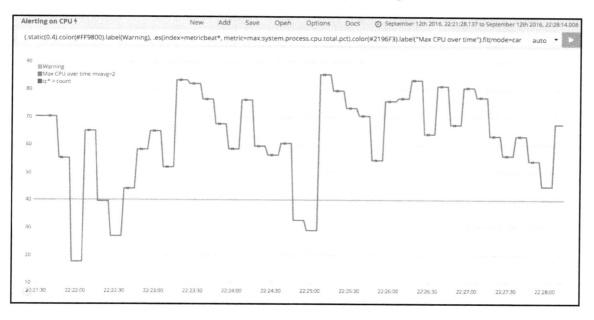

Maximum system CPU with alert spotted

Now, as you can see, I can clearly see all the problematic values, and can be certain that an alert has been triggered and a proactive action may have been taken.

Summary

In this chapter, we have seen how we can use Kibana in the context of technical metric analytics. We relied on the data that Metricbeat is able to ship from a machine and visualized the result both in Kibana Dashboard and in Kibana Timelion. In the next chapter, we will stay in the land of metric analytics, but will use a business use case: the United States domestic flights use case.

6
Graph Exploration in Kibana

In earlier chapters, we went through a logging and metric analytics scenario that mainly leveraged the aggregation API in Elasticsearch.

But what if the need was not necessarily to highlight the KPI in the data, but rather to show the interconnection of data based on relevancy? This is where Elastic Graph comes into play. Graph is an X-Pack plugin that allows us to reveal significant connections between data indexed in Elasticsearch.

Elastic Graph comes with a new API in Elasticsearch and a new UI in Kibana, which offers a totally different approach to exploring data: rather than addressing data through the angle of value aggregation and narrowing them down by filtering to discover patterns, Graph allows you to play with vertices (the terms indexed in Elasticsearch) and connections (how many documents share the terms in the index) and map out significant relations.

In this chapter, we'll learn the following concepts of the Elastic Graph flow:

- Differentiating Elastic Graph from traditional graph technologies out there, not from a competitive perspective but rather as a technological comparison, and looking at the challenges that Elastic Graph tries to solve.
- Stack Overflow use case: Analyzing the data structure, and tring different graph explorations, from a simple exploration that uses the default settings and a limited set of term, to a more advanced one that includes more than one terms and leverages some of the fundamental settings of the Elastic Graph API

Introducing the basics of Elastic Graph

Elastic Graph was created to reveal significant relations between data, so that we can see how the variables in question interact. It forms recommendations based on these relations. Data is highly connected, either implicitly or explicitly. These connections can be represented as a graph. Graph based data analysis provides unique insights based on the use case:

- In a search use case, using a graph, the search experience could be enhanced if the user gets related content based on the query they submitted. This is typically what we could see on an e-commerce website; for example, when purchasing a phone, you could get related accessories. But in the context of Elasticsearch, based on the click stream on a website, the user could get real-time, relevant, and significant suggestions based on his purchase behavior.

- In the security analytics use case, suspicious connections could be proactively detected based on the logged data. If we have all the access logs for an application such as firewall logs, proxy logs, and front-end and back-end logs, Elastic Graph could be used to correlate data between all these layers and trace down user activities. All connections could be associated with an IP address, and, thus, if suspicious, index of banned IP addresses could be built.

- In a business analytics use case, such as financial services, Elastic Graph could be used to represent the financial transaction between bank accounts or entities, with the aim of forensically detecting fraud. If for example, the idea is to monitor transactions between accounts, maybe 1 transaction of a millions dollars is not suspicious, but a million transactions of one dollar between 2 accounts could be. Using Elastic Graph, we could highlight such behavior and extend fraud detection to all connected accounts.

The preceding examples are just a subset of what would be possible. To understand how they could be implemented, I'm going to go through the fundamental differences between the usual graph technologies and Elastic Graph.

How Elastic Graph is different from other graph technologies out there

It's important to understand how Elastic Graph differs from other graph technologies. There are multiple differences. The first one relates to the way that the data are modelled in a typical graph database; the following diagram gives an example of this:

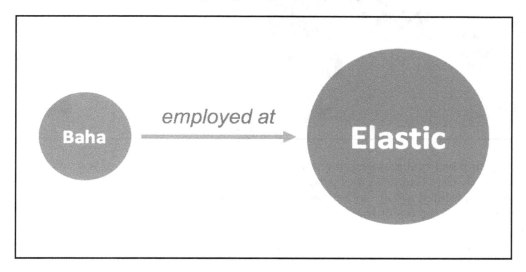

The preceding diagram is an illustration of the graph concept that models the relation between **Baha** and **Elastic**. The size of each vertex can depend on the number of vertex connection. In the example above, the **Elastic** vertex might have more connections than the **Baha** vertex. The graph is composed of vertices (the **circles**) and a relation (**arrow**). Each entity could have attributes, such as the arrow here, which has the **employed at** attribute.

In traditional graph technologies, the preceding model would be written synchronously, then the user will be able to explore it. There won't be any notion of relevancy in what the user explores: this is exactly what Elastic Graph doesn't provide.

Elastic Graph will create and show relevant and significant relations based on index data.

Here is an diagram to illustrate what happens in common graph technologies:

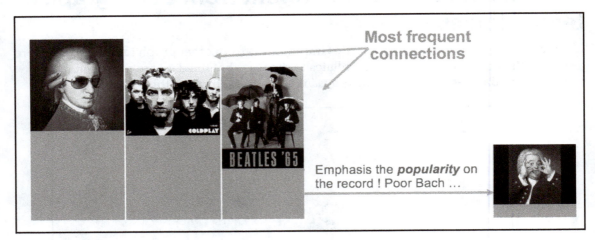

In some graph technologies search results are based on the popularity of records, so that if we take music data that describes people and what they listen to, and try to search for **Mozart** to get related artists, we will get the preceding results. For the sake of simplicity I have represented the result rows in the form of green boxes, with the related artist on top of if. The bigger the green box, the more popular the artist. In our search example, the first row will naturally be Mozart, but then we'll find Coldplay, the Beatles, and somewhere at the end we would find Bach.

Coldplay and the Beatles are pretty popular across the dataset, and they will most likely be present in every single graph exploration. Their popularity is diluting the signal we are looking for, classical music artists related to Mozart; they are creating noise. They are called super connected entities because data points are never more than a couple of hops away from them; they will always end up touching a super connected entity, as shown in the following figure:

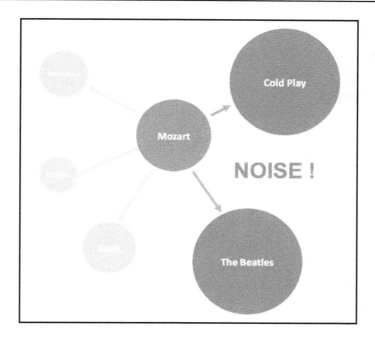

Their inclusion is usually what happens in a mainstream graphing technology, just because it's not their job to calculate the relevancy and the significance of the results.

The good news is it's exactly what Elastic Graph is good at.

 When we throw terms in the Elasticsearch indices, it naturally knows which data are the most interesting, and leverages that to build the graph.

Elasticsearch looks for the reinforcement of many documents to show the strength/relevancy of the connection.

 Elastic Graph could show you an awfully large number of things, but Elasticsearch shows the most relevant first, which is what the significant links algorithm is doing.

The following picture illustrates the concept of noise detection in a graph:

In the preceding illustration, we can see what happens when a user searches for Mozart:

- Some records, such as those by Mozart, will make a significant move towards the top of the results on the left. This would happen to Bach, Beethoven, Verdi, and so on.
- Some records, such as those by Coldplay, will barely move. The same would happen to Pink Floyd, the Beatles, and others.

This is how Elastic Graph differentiates between the first population of data (the signal) and the second slow moving and less relevant population (the noise). Only the signal would be presented to the user, as the following graph shows:

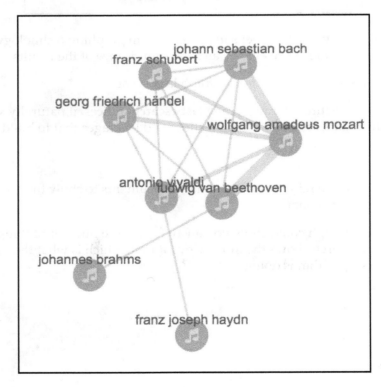

It's now time to explore some more of the features of Elastic Graph through the example of the Stack Overflow dataset.

Exploring the Stack Overflow dataset with Elastic Graph

Stack Overflow is a website widely used to ask and answer questions about a very large set of topics in the computer science industry. It's a perfect resource to try out Elastic Graph, as the data it holds will contain users who are connected to questions, answers, tags, comments, and so on. In this section, we'll index the Stack Overflow dataset in Elasticsearch, look at the structure of the data, and build relations using Elastic Graph.

Prepare to graph!

The dataset we will use is located in the source attached to this book in the Chapter 6 folder. You will find a ZIP file called `StackOverflow4Graph.zip` that contains the following files:

- `IndexPosts.py`: Python script that indexes the data in your Elasticsearch cluster
- `Posts.csv`: The dataset itself
- `readme.txt`: The readme file, which, by the way, contains a link to a tweet that illustrates what we are going to do in this part

The following example gives an idea of Stack Overflow Graph exploration and also why popularity based connections show less relevant results.

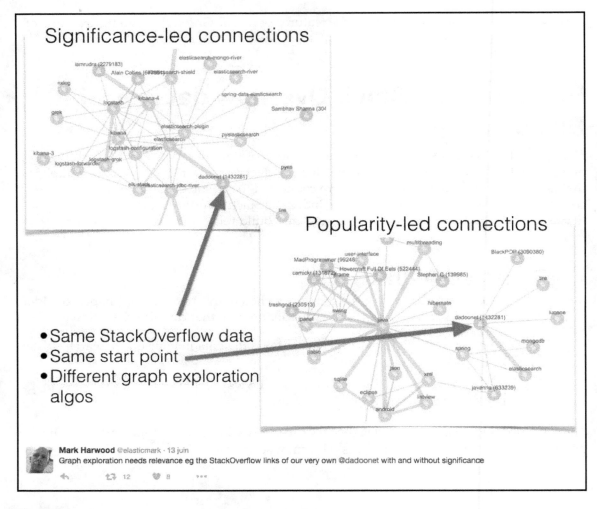

We'll first extract the ZIP file and execute the Python script to index the data in Elasticsearch. The script expects three arguments:

- Elasticsearch hostname
- Elasticsearch user name
- Elasticsearch password

With your Elasticsearch cluster running, issue the following command line:

```
pythonIndexPosts.py ELASTICSEARCH_HOSTNAME USERNAME PASSWORD
```

You will need to check if the data has been indexed, in the console, for example:

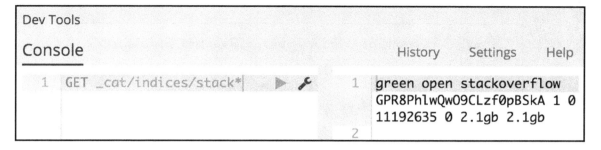

In the above screenshot, we can see on the right side of the console that **1192635** documents have been indexed. Let's now see what the data looks like.

The data structure

No specific data structure need to be created in Elasticsearch to use Elastic Graph, as Elastic Graph works with the terms you indexed. Before graphing the Stack Overflow data, we'll examine the structure the data. To do so, you first need to create an index pattern in Kibana that will be used by the Elastic Graph plugin as well.

Go to the **management/index patterns** section and create the Stack Overflow **index pattern**, as shown here:

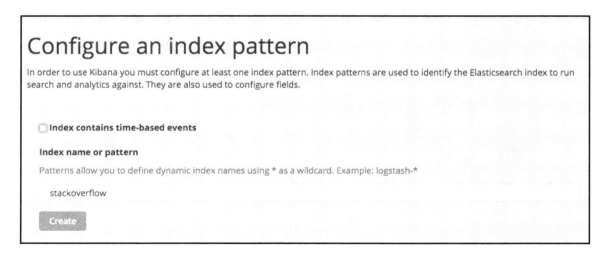

Once created, just go into the **Discover** tab and expand a random document. This will look similar to the following:

```
▼   tag: javascript, jquery  user: learnmore (1742289),
    ckoverflow  _score: 1


    Table    JSON

     1 ▾  {
     2       "_index": "stackoverflow",
     3       "_type": "qna",
     4       "_id": "AVgSYpTT1vXMTQ2oWJCN",
     5       "_score": 1,
     6 ▾     "_source": {
     7 ▾       "tag": [
     8           "javascript",
     9           "jquery"
    10         ],
    11 ▾       "user": [
    12           "learnmore (1742289)",
    13           "Vohuman (848164)"
    14         ]
    15       }
    16  }
```

The document has a fairly simple structure. It contains two arrays:

- **tag**: The topic of the questions
- **user**: The user involved in the questions

From there, we can start to explore our data, starting with a *simple exploration*.

Simple exploration

Before exploring the data, I'll describe Elastic Graph. The components of the graph menu are shown as follows:

As you can see from the preceding screenshot, there are four parts of the graph menu:

- A combo to choose the index to be explored.
- A plus button, which will walk you through choosing fields to use as vertices in the graph.
- An input to issue queries for filtering the graph.
- A toolbar to manage the workspace, where the graph is created, opened, and saved. The Elastic Graph 5.0 UI isn't so different from that of 2.x, but some notable enhancements have been included, such as this toolbar. You can now save a graph exploration and open it later as you would for a dashboard. This gives you the potential to configure drill-downs for a given workspace to switch from a graph visualization to underlying data through a URL. The URL can be dynamic; we'll illustrate this feature in this first exploration.

To start the exploration, we'll select the `stackoverflow` index pattern and use the `tag` field, as shown in the following image :

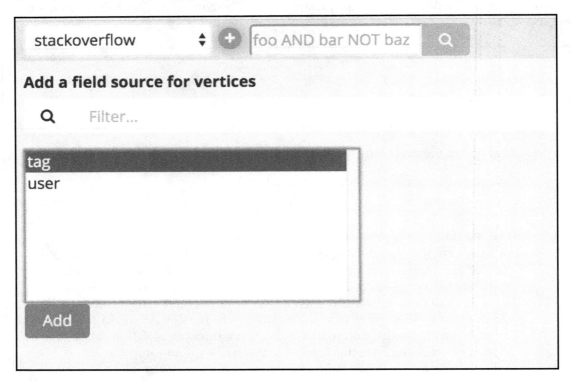

Add the tag and search for something in the query input.

Let's start by searching for `elasticsearch` and see the following result that is displayed:

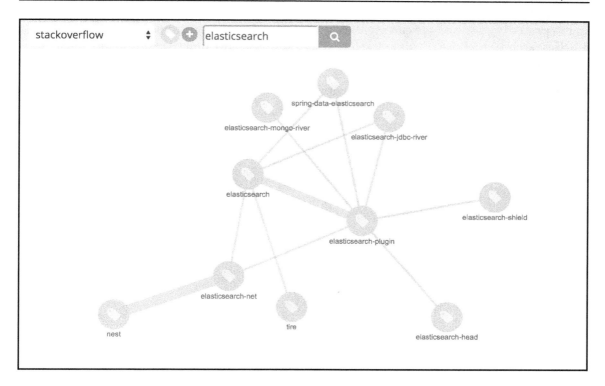

The graph contains vertices (the **yellow circles**) representing the tags, and connections between the vertices representing the number of documents sharing the term. For example, if we select the connection from the vertex nest, we will see the following statistics:

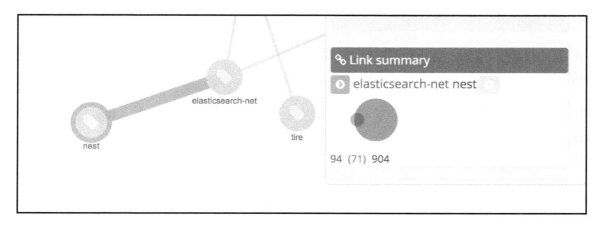

In the preceding picture, we can see that, within the **94** documents that contain the term **elasticsearch-net**, **71** also contain the term nest, which totally makes sense as long as we know that nest is the .Net client for Elasticsearch.

During our exploration, a context menu appears on the right of the workspace:

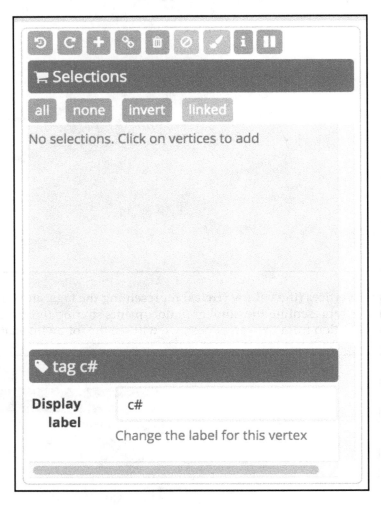

This menu offers some actions, such as a plus button to expand the selection of a term in the graph. If you try this button at the current state of our exploration, then you will get the following:

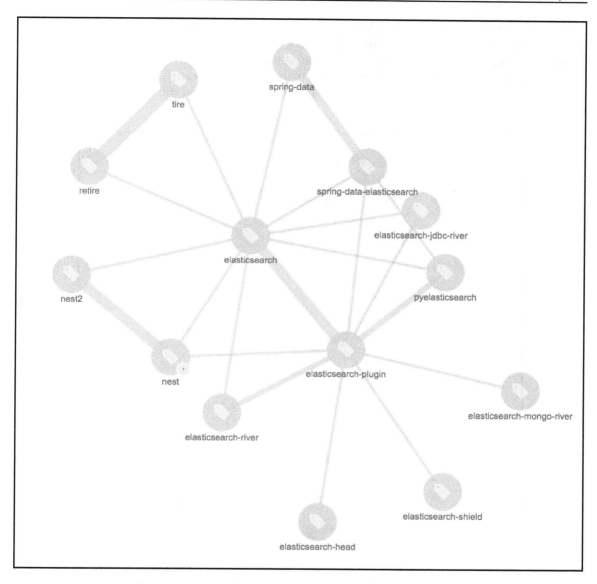

In the same menu, the first two buttons allow you to cancel and redo actions, enabling you to go back and forth in the exploration. You can try to cancel the expansion that we just opened; you should be brought back to the first version of our graph. Redo it to see the previous graph again.

Another button you can use is the **Delete** button. This will remove a vertex in the current workspace; data are not removed from the index. This vertex can be retrieved in a future exploration, which is different from the **Blacklist** button next to it which blacklists the vertex from the current workspace-in other words, it won't appear anymore in your exploration. Let's, for example, blacklist the elasticsearch 'river' in the exploration as river has been deprecated for a while now:

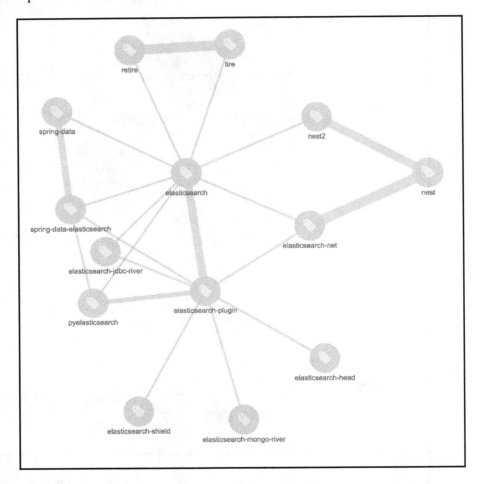

You can also, if you want, customize the color of a vertex in the graph, such as the **elasticsearch** term here, which is kind of the center of this graph:

If you click multiple times on the plus button, a lot of terms will appear on the workspace, expanding the graph with the next group of relevant terms, making the graph layout swing and float until all terms have been placed properly on the screen. To freeze the layout, you can use the play/pause button.

There are two final possible actions: the Add links button we will see in the advanced exploration, and the drill-down globally button, which displays the available drill down actions, as shown in the following image:

In the preceding example, the only available drill down is **Raw documents**, which essentially means that, whichever vertex you select, you will be able to see all the documents containing the terms. The following image shows how the drill down works to get raw documents:

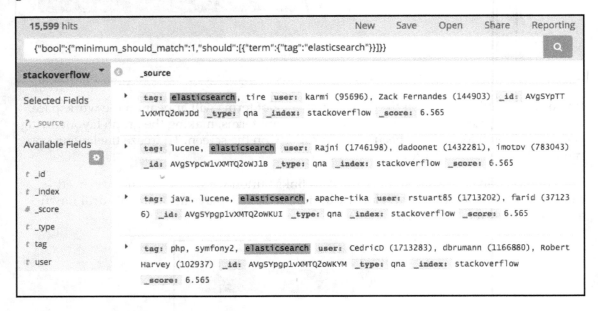

In the preceding example, we drilled down into the raw documents that contain Elasticsearch. But what if I want to get a list of questions around a specific topic? This is where drill down gets even more interesting. If you go to the workspace settings and click on the **Drill-Downs** section, you will see that you can set a URL that will be opened when you drill down:

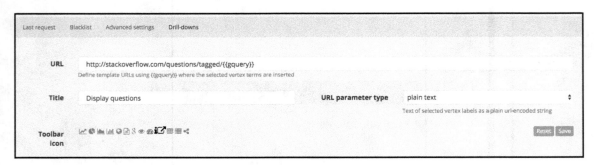

In the preceding screenshot, I've set the URL to be
`http://stackoverflow.com/questions/tagged/{{gquery}}`, where `gquery` is the actual term content. This means that, if I drill down in a tag, it should redirect me to the page that lists the question related to that tag. For example, if I create a graph for Kibana and select the **kibana** vertex in the graph to drill down to, we'll get the following options:

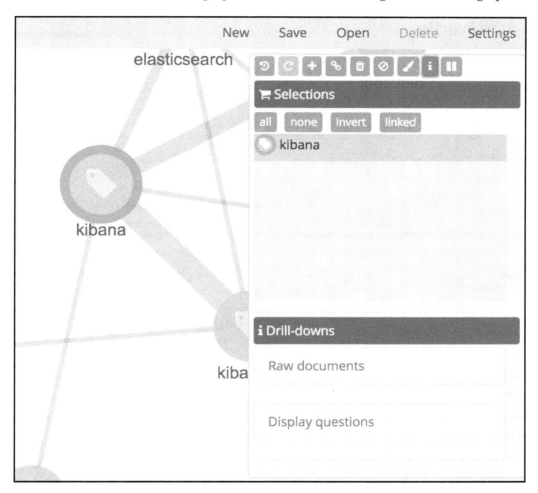

There is also provision to access Kibana questions on Stack Overflow. If you click on **Display questions**, you will be redirected to the following page:

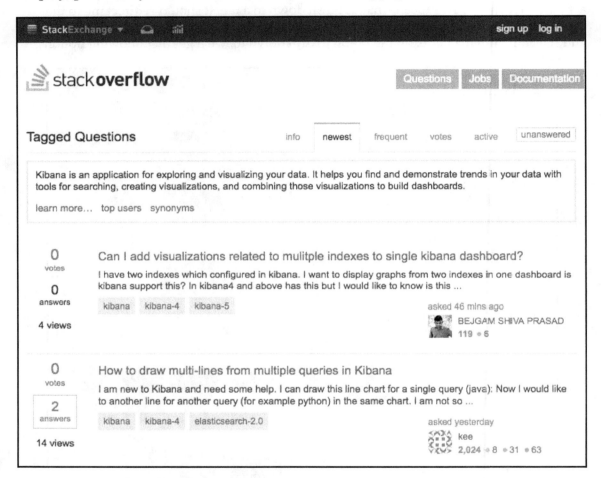

In this section, we went through a simple exploration based on one term in the document. We will see in the next section that exploration can get more advanced, and also play with the graph settings a bit.

Advanced exploration

In this section, we'll use Elastic Graph to see the impact of the significant links setting, try to connect different sets of data, and finally use the drill down feature to build a bridge between Elastic Graph and the Kibana dashboards.

Disabling significant links

Firstly, using the graph that we created in the previous section, we will examine the concept of super connected entities by disabling the **Significant links** algorithm used to remove the noise so that only the signal is displayed, as shown here:

Sample size	2000
	Terms are identified from samples of the most relevant documents. Bigger is not necessarily better - can be slower and less relevant.
	☐ Significant links
	Identify terms that are "significant" rather than simply popular
Certainty	3
	The min number of documents that are required as evidence before introducing a related term
Diversity field	[No diversification] ⬍
	To avoid document samples being dominated by a single voice, pick the field that helps identify the source of bias. *This must be a single-term field or searches will be rejected with an error*
Timeout (ms)	5000
	Max time in milliseconds a request can run

If we clear the workspace from its current graph with the Remove button and search for elasticsearch again, you should get the following graph with **significant links** disabled:

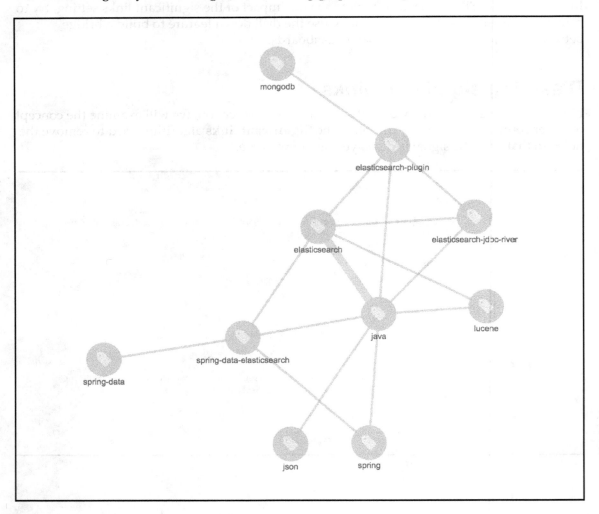

Some of the entities we see in the graph are not obvious super connected entities, but others are, such as Java (Elasticsearch is first written in Java and widely used in Java projects), Lucene (Elasticsearch is built on top of Lucene), JSON (data is stored in the form of a JSON document in Elasticsearch), and so on. So you can see the difference compared to the first graph we built in the previous section: This graph is built based on the popularity of the terms rather than their relevance.

Multi-term graph exploration

In this example, we'll try to put ourselves in the shoes of a recruiter, and look for a Stack Overflow user that is involved in different topics. For our example, we'll look for the most significant relationship for users involved in apache spark and apache kafka topics. To do so, click the plus sign next to the index picker and add the user field as shown in the following image:

We first want to show our tags and then look for users that touch both topics, so disable the user field for this first search by holding down **Shift** and clicking on the field icon:

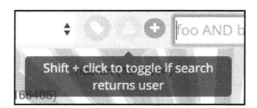

Search for Spark. You should get the following graph, from which we just want to keep the **apache-spark** term and **apache-kafka**. Select them, invert the selection, and remove the nodes to get the change shown here:

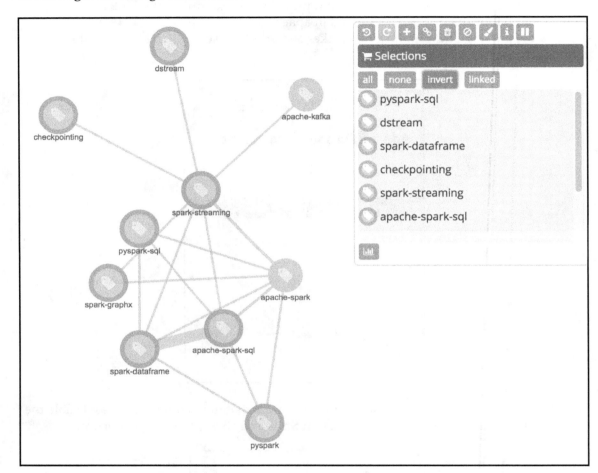

Now we need to disable the tag field and re-enable the user tag. Once you have done that, click on **apache-spark-sql** and start clicking on the Plug button in the contextual menu to make any involved users appear. When there are no more users, do the same for **apache-spark**. You should end up with the following result for **apache kafka**:

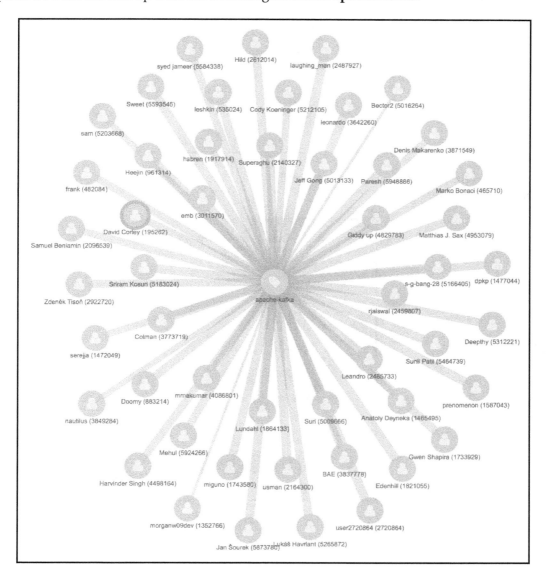

You should get the same kind of graph for **apache-spark**. Two sets of terms are now displayed; we want to group them so they represent Spark users and Kafka users. Click on either the **apache-spark** term or **apache-kafka** and click on **linked** to select the linked vertices. Clicking on the link button will give you the following result:

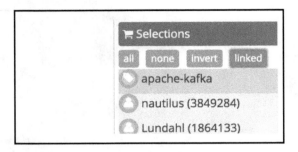

In the vertices list, click on **apache-kafka** and then click on **group** at the bottom to **group** the buttons as shown here:

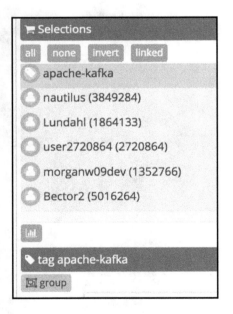

If you proceed the same way for **apache-spark**, you should get the following workspace:

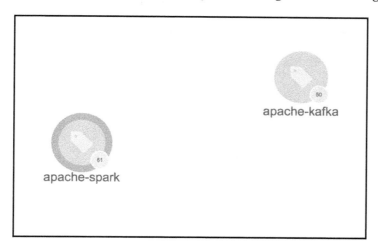

Now, to connect both, we first need to select both groups by holding *SHIFT*, and then clicking on the buttons, as shown here:

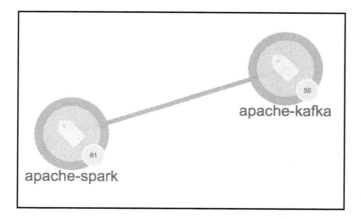

If you click on each group, you should see an **ungroup** button located in the same place as the on-board option. Ungroup them, and let's see the results:

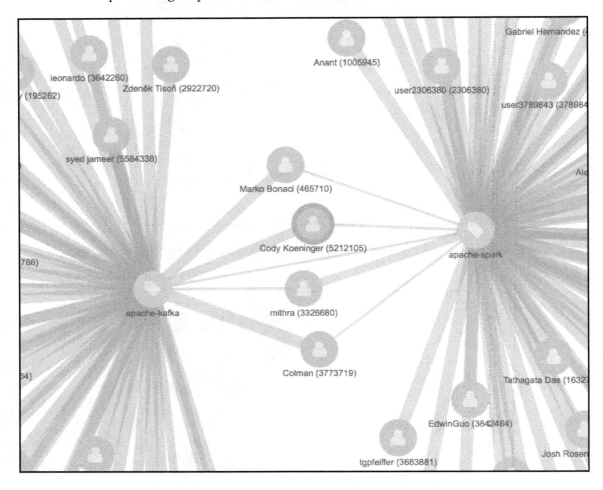

Remember our job here: We are looking for a user profile involved in both Spark and Kafka discussions. Fine; we have four of them. In the next section, we will see how we can use Elastic Graph to create a second filter and narrow down our selection.

Advanced drill-downs

The real power of drill downs is apparent when used in conjunction with a kibana visualization. Here, we'll create a bar chart visualization that shows the top 10 topics:

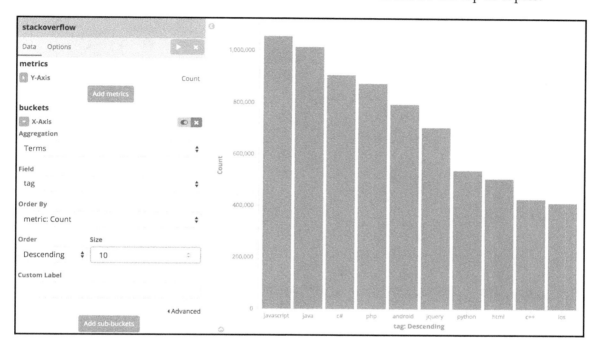

What is interesting here is the visualization URL. Copy and paste it in a new drill down option in our graph. Link to the new visualization, as shown here:

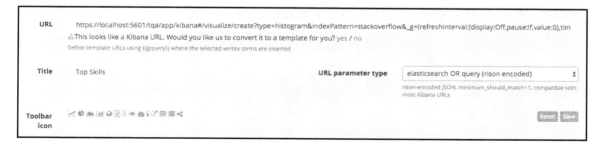

The setting detects that it's probably a Kibana URL, and offers to convert the URL to a template. Click on yes so that the {{gquery}} template will be placed properly, and save the new drill down option. Try the new drill down option for each user in your graph:

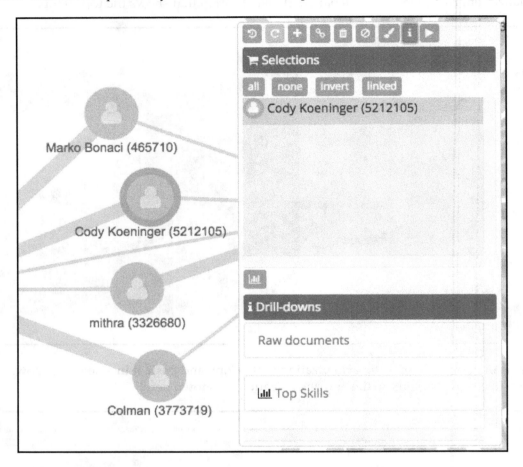

Finally, our expectations in terms of profile sourcing have changed just a little bit. We want to find a profile that is involved in both Spark and Kafka, but also has some visualization development skills with d3.js.

One of the preceding users fulfills our requirements, and has the following skills profile:

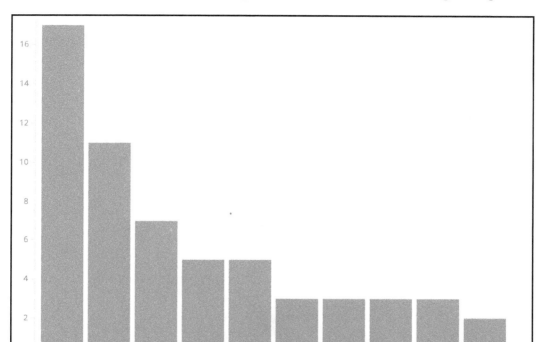

Summary

In this chapter, we have seen the difference between industry Graph technologies and what Elastic Graph provides. Elastic Graph ties up aggregation and relevancy features to connect the document in Elasticsearch. Through this process, users get a way to build recommendations out of the indexed content. We then looked at some examples that illustrate how Elastic Graph can be used through simple exploration up to advanced exploration with multi-term graphs and advanced drill-downs.

In the next chapter, we'll start to delve fairly deeply into the world of Kibana customization by implementing an extension for Timelion.

7
Customizing Kibana 5.0 Timelion

In the previous chapters, we went through the holistic visualization experience that Kibana offers through all the different plugins, paying particular attention to the following features:

- The dashboard plugin, which, historically, was the first way to visualize data in Kibana
- The graph plugin, which helps you visualize connections within your data
- The Timelion plugin, which enables the visualization of time series data
- Visualization as part of the Kibana dashboard
- Expression in Timelion

If you want to get more out of Kibana, such as visualizing data in a type of chart that does not exist in standard palettes, or even finding another way to manipulate data, you can decide to extend the capabilities of existing palettes or build your own plugin. A good candidate for extension is Timelion.

Timelion has a plugin-driven architecture, in the sense that the existing function collection can be very easily extended. In this chapter, we'll write our own extension to pull data from Google Analytics Reporting API (GARA). The reason for this is that Kibana not only provides a streamlined visualization experience on top of Elasticsearch, but can also be extended to become a centralized visualization platform.

Kibana has been built using AngularJS 1.4.7, which means that extending `Timelion` requires you to write JavaScript code. Hopefully, we won't need to understand the complexity of the Kibana architecture there, and will only focus on the implementation and integration logic.

Diving into Timelion code

Understanding how a Kibana plugin is structured is essential to tackle the development of extensions. This is what we'll look at first before diving into the `Timelion` function's code.

Understanding the Kibana plugin structure

A Kibana plugin is fundamentally an Angular application; it follows a specific structure, that is, a layout, as shown next:

```
public
app-logo.png
app.js server
api.js
index.js
gulpfile.js
package.json
README.md
```

- The `public` folder contains all the public files that will be served to the user's browser, except the `app.js` file, which is used to load the following:
  - All the application UI components and libraries
  - All the routes that the backend API will serve
- The `server` folder contains all the backend files, which implement the API called by the front end code. Typically, the routes defined in the `app.js` file will point to that API. Note that this folder could have a different name.
- The `index.js` file is used to bootstrap the application and essentially manage and run the required plugin life cycle steps.
- The `gulpfile.js` file is a configuration for Gulp, the preferred build system for Kibana.
- The `package.json` file contains the project description, along with development and project dependencies.
- The `README.md` file contains plugin documentation.

As with every other Kibana plugin, Timelion follows the preceding structure. What we are going to extend is a part of the backend code, essentially the code within the `server` folder, which will be used in the UI.

If we go to the `Timelion` repository at `https://github.com/elastic/kibana/tree/maste r/src/core_plugins/timelion` server and we look at the `server` folder, here is what we get:

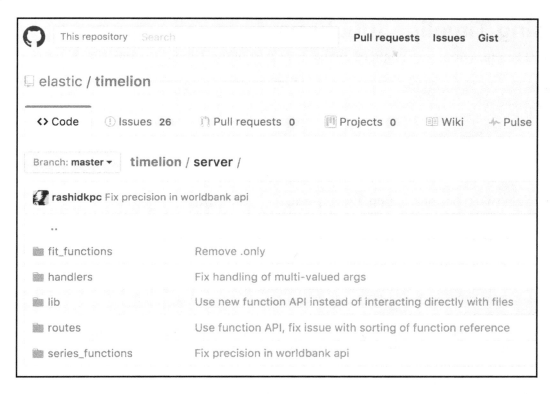

Timelion server folder structure

There are five folders here:

- The `routes` folder, which contains the API-exposed HTTP, called by the UI side (public folder)
- The `lib` folder, which contains the core Timelion framework
- The `handlers` folder, which contains the `Timelion expression` function handlers
- The `series_functions` folder, which contains all the functions available in the `Timelion expression`
- The `fit_functions` folder, which contains a specific set of functions used to fit data in a chart where data is missing

In this book, we want to create a new function, that will be available as a part of the `Timelion` function, so the `series_functions` folder is the place to explore.

Using Timelion functions

`Timelion` functions are functions available as part of the Timelion expression builder.

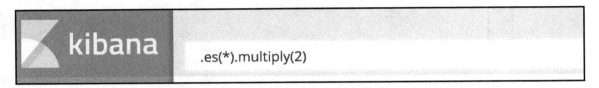

There are two types of function, the implementations of which can be found here: `https://github.com/elastic/kibana core_plugins/timelion/server/lib/classes`.

- `Datasource`: These functions point to a data source and are usually used to start expressions, such as `es()`, `quandl()`, `graphite()`, and so on
- `Chainable`: These are functions that work on the data returned by the `data source`, such as `multiply()`, `derivates()`, and so on

We'll see later in this chapter that what we want to create is a new data source that fetches data from the Google Analytics Reporting API and returns a series list, which will be rendered by Timelion.

We can take the `worldbank` function as an example to analyze the structure of a data source:

```
...
module.exports = new Datasource ('worldbank', {
  args: [
    {
      name: 'code', // countries/all/indicators/SP.POP.TOTL
      types: ['string', 'null'],
      help: '...'
    }
  ],
  aliases: ['wb'],
  help: '...',
  fn: function worldbank(args, tlConfig) {
    var config = _.defaults(args.byName, {
      code: 'countries/wld/indicators/SP.POP.TOTL'
```

```
    });
    var time = {
      min: moment(tlConfig.time.from).format('YYYY'),
      max:  moment(tlConfig.time.to).format('YYYY')
    };
    var URL = 'http://api.worldbank.org/' + config.code +
      '?date=' + time.min + ':' + time.max +
      '&format=json' +
      '&per_page=1000';
    return fetch(URL).then(function (resp) { return resp.json();
}).then(function (resp) {
        var hasData = false;
        var respSeries = resp[1];
        var deduped = {};
        var description;
        _.each (respSeries, function (bucket) {
          if (bucket.value != null) hasData = true;
          description = bucket.country.value + ' ' +
bucket.indicator.value;
          deduped[bucket.date] = bucket.value;
        });
        var data = _.compact(_.map(deduped, function (val, date) {
          // Discard nulls
          if (val == null) return;
          return [moment(date, 'YYYY').valueOf(), parseInt(val, 10)];
        }));
        if (!hasData) throw new Error('Worldbank request succeeded, but
there was no data for ' + config.code);
        return {
          type: 'seriesList',
          list: [{
            data:  data,
            type: 'series',
            label: description,
            _meta: {
              worldbank_request: URL
            }
          }]
        };
      }).catch(function (e) {
        throw e;
      });
    }
  });
```

I've removed some parts from the preceding snippet. You can find the full version at `https://github.com/elastic/kibana/blob/master/src/cor e_plugins/timelion/server/series_functions/worldbank.js`.

The aforementioned code exports a data source module, which is composed of the following:

- Arguments: These denote the arguments to pass to the function. Each of these has a name, a type, and the argument description. If the type's `array` contains null, it means that the argument can be optional.
- Aliases: These are used instead of the full function names. For example, the alias `wb` can be used instead of the full function name `worldbank`.
- Help: This provides the function description.
- Function: This denotes the `data source` function, which has been described by the aforementioned arguments, and the `Timelion configuration` variable, which contains all the context variables.

So essentially, a function is composed of its functional description and implementation. If you dig a little deeper into the implementation here, you will notice a few things.

Firstly, the arguments are browsed and set to a default value of null within the `_.defaults(args.byName, ....)` functions. This gives the user the option not to pass all the optional arguments, and it is something we'll use in the implementation of our extension.

Another option is the ability to get the current selected timeframe in the Kibana time-picker component, shown here:

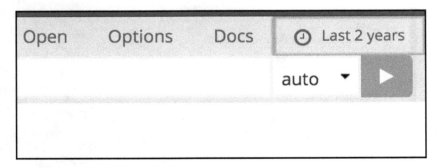

Kibana Time picker

This is where the `Timelion config` variable comes into play; both the start (`tlConfig.time.from`) and the end (`tlConfig.time.to`) values are in this object.

Once we have both the argument and the time frame, the code is ready to call the `worldbank` API by building the API URL in the `URL` variable. The fetch function is used to call the API and fetch the data from the `worldbank` API.

The last step is to format the data so that Timelion is able to parse and render it. The convention in Timelion is to return a series list, as follows:

```
{
  type: 'seriesList',
  list: [{
   data:  data,
   type: 'series',
   label: description,
   _meta: {
     worldbank_request: URL
   }
  }]
};
```

From what we see in the aforementioned code, the `worldbank` function can only return a series list that contains a single series. This is an important feature that we'll use in our implementation. The series contains a type, a label, and an array of tuple-called data, which should be structured as follows:

```
[ ['timestamp_1', 'numeric_value_1'] , ... , ['timestamp_n',
'numeric_value_n']]
```

The tuples should have a timestamp and a numeric value, which will be used to draw the points on the chart.

This is all we need to understand in order to implement our first extension. It's pretty straightforward: Describe the function, gather the arguments and the time frame, call the external API, and finally format the response to fit Timelion expectations.

When Google Analytics meets the lion

Google Analytics Reporting API (GARA) is a part of the Google API library, and offers hooks to get the data coming from website traffic, which one can retrieve as part of Google Analytics visualizations, such as the following:

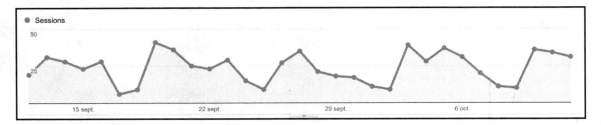

Google analytics sessions over time

What if we could centralize our site analytics in a single visualization application? This is exactly what Timelion brings to Kibana-the possibility to fetch data from external data, other than Elasticsearch. In this section, we'll set up the development environment to implement an extension for GARA. Then we'll set up our Google API account and finally implement the function.

Setting up our development environment

Implementing a `Timelion` function requires you to install a couple of tools, starting with Nodejs 4.6.0 (`https://nodejs.org/en`). Download the appropriate package, depending on your OS, and run the installation. Nodejs is the backend on which Kibana runs. When you download Kibana on elastic.co, you don't need to think about it, but in development mode you need nodejs in order to have total control over the runtime life cycle.

Once installed, you need to install Gulp on your system. To do so, run the following command in a shell, as described at `https://github.com/gulpjs/gulp/blob/master/docs/getting-started.md`.

```
npm install --global gulp-cli
```

This will install Gulp, which we will use to do the following:

- Synchronize our extension with the `Kibana source` folder, which means that every time you make a change the code is synced and Kibana is restarted
- Build our extension and package it

We now need first to clone the Kibana project and then to clone the Timelion extension project. You will see that the project already contains the implementation, for the sake of simplicity. I'll explain each part of it.

You need to have Git CLI installed in order to clone the repositories. If this is not already the case, then follow documentation found at
`https://git-scm.com/book/en/v2/Getting-Started-Installing-Git`.

Once installed, issue the following command to clone the Kibana repository:

```
git clone https://github.com/elastic/kibana.git
```

By default, the master branch is the code available as part of the clone repository; the extension I've built for the book was implemented for Kibana v5.0.0-beta1, so we'll use this version, with the help of tags:

```
git checkout tags/v5.0.0-beta1
```

The preceding code will switch the code state from master to beta1. Clone the extension repository at this level in your file system:

```
Git clone https://github.com/bahaaldine/timelion-google-analytics.git
```

You should now have the following directory structure:

```
$ pwd
kibana timelion-google-analytics
```

Now we need to download the dependencies for each project. Issue the following command in both folders:

```
npm install
```

This will download all the `Javascript` libraries needed to run Kibana and build the extension.

Running Kibana v5.0.0-beta1 also means that you will need to run Elasticsearch v5.0.0-beta1, which can be downloaded at
`https://www.elastic.co/downloads/past-releases/elasticsearch-5-0-0-beta1`.
Download, install, and run Elasticsearch as described at the beginning of this book.

Verifying our installation

Now that everything is set up, we need to configure Kibana in order to simplify our developer life. You might have noticed that when you install a plugin in Kibana it takes a certain time, sometimes a couple of minutes. That's because Kibana optimizes the code contained in the plugin. In our case, it could be even worse; potentially we could get this optimization step triggered each time we make a change in our codeâ⊚⊚not an option.

This is why you will need to add the following settings to the Kibana configuration file (`kibana/config/kibana.yml`):

```
optimize:
sourceMaps: '#cheap-source-map' # options ->
http://webpack.github.io/docs/configuration.html#devtool
unsafeCache: true
lazyPrebuild: false
```

This way, the optimization step will essentially be shortened for the sake of rapid development.

You are ready to launch everything:

1. First launch Elasticsearch.
2. Then launch Kibana.
3. Finally, launch the following commands in the `timelion-google-analytics` folder:

```
gulp sync
gulp dev
```

The first command allows you to sync the extension code base in the `sibling kibana installation` folder; the directive is defined in the `gulpfile.js`:

```
gulp.task('sync', function(done) {
  syncPluginTo(kibanaPluginDir, done);
});
```

In the preceding code, `kibanaPluginDir` is `../kibana5.0.0-beta1`.

The second command opens a sync pipe between the two folders so that, every time you modify a file in the extension, Gulp will propagate the changes to Kibana.

Now that everything runs, open your browser and go to `http://localhost:5601`, then switch to Timelion and check that the `.ganalytics` expression is available:

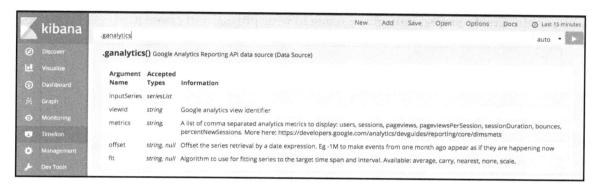

ganalytis expression in Timelion

From there, we'll need to configure your Google API account.

Setting up our Google API account

The following steps allow an application to fetch data from GARA:

1. Create a Google API project.
2. Enable the Analytics Reporting API.
3. Configure access from the IAM console.
4. Add a new user to Google Analytics authorized users.

Let's start by creating a **Google APIs** project from
`https://console.developers.google.com`:

Create a Google API project

Click on the **Create project** link, give a name to your project, and create it:

Creation popup

Once the project is created, we need to enable the API we would like to use by clicking on the **ENABLE API** button:

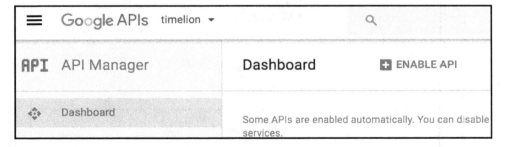

Enable API button

In our case, our preferred API is the `Google Analytics Reporting API`:

Search for Google Analytics Reporting API

Click on the **ENABLE** API button:

Enable API button

Now we are ready to tackle the security features. We need first to create a service account to allow server-to-server communication between the Kibana Nodejs server and the Google API servers. To do so, open
`https://console.developers.google.com/iam-admin/serviceaccounts`.

A popup will appear. You will need to select the newly created project. The list of current service accounts will appear (it should be empty); click on the **CREATE SERVICE ACCOUNT** button:

🛡 IAM & Admin	Service Accounts ➕ CREATE SERVICE ACCOUNT

Create service account button

You should just have to pass a service account name, pick the owner role, and check Furnish a new private key, selecting the JSON option:

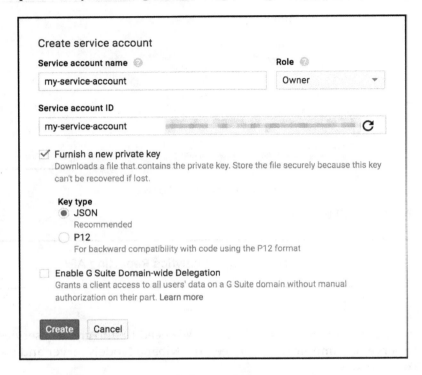

Service account wizard

Click on the **Create** button, and this should trigger the download of a JSON file containing the following structure:

```
{
    "type": "service_account",
    "project_id": " ... PROJECT ID ... ",
    "private_key_id": " ... PRIVATE ID ... ",
    "private_key": " ... PRIVATE KEY ... ",
    "client_email": " ... CLIENT EMAIL ... ",
    "client_id": " ... CLIENT ID ... ",
    "auth_uri": " ... AUTH URI ... ",
    "token_uri": " ... TOKEN URI ...   ",
    "auth_provider_x509_cert_url": " ... AUTH PROVIDER X509 CERT
        URL ... ",
    "client_x509_cert_url": " ... CLIENT X509 CERT URL ...  "
}
```

We need to pass this key to Kibana to be able to call GARA from the extension. There is a file configuration in the Timelion directory. Go to the `Kibana installation` directory and open `timelion.jon` located in the `Timelion source` directory:

```
$ cd kibana5.0.0-beta1/
$ cd src/core_plugins/timelion/
$ pwd
/Users/bahaaldine/Dropbox/elastic/plugins/kibana/kibana5.0.0-
beta1/src/core_plugins/timelion
$ ls
bower.json bower_components index.js init.js package.json public server
timelion.json vendor_components
```

Open the file and the key to the file in line with the following structure:

```
{
  "quandl": {
    "key": "someKeyHere"
  },
  "es": {
    "timefield": "@timestamp",
    "default_index": "_all"
  },
  "graphite": {
    "url": "https://www.hostedgraphite.com/UID/ACCESS_KEY/graphite"
  },
  "default_rows": 2,
  "default_columns": 2,
  "max_buckets": 2000,
  "target_buckets": 200,
  "google": {
    "service_account": {
      "type": "service_account",
      "project_id": " ... PROJECT ID ... ",
      "private_key_id": " ... PRIVATE ID ... ",
      "private_key": " ... PRIVATE KEY ... ",
      "client_email": " ... CLIENT EMAIL ... ",
      "client_id": " ... CLIENT ID ... ",
      "auth_uri": " ... AUTH URI ... ",
      "token_uri": " ... TOKEN URI ... ",
      "auth_provider_x509_cert_url": " ... AUTH PROVIDER X509 CERT
        URL ... ",
      "client_x509_cert_url": " ... CLIENT X509 CERT URL ... "
  }
    }
  }
```

After saving the file, the Kibana server will automatically restart. You should then get the following log line in the Kibana logs:

```
restarting server due to changes in
"src/core_plugins/timelion/timelion.json"
```

The last step of this configuration part is to add the newly created service account to the authorized user in the Google Analytics console. The user is identified by the client_email in your JSON private key. Look at the online documentation found at https://support.google.com/analytics/answer/1009702?hl=en#Add. You will essentially need to access the user management console within Google Analytics and add a user there.

Verifying our configuration

If you finalize the preceding steps, you should be able to use the expression in Timelion. For that, you'll need a Google Analytics view identifier that identifies a report. In my case, here is what I have from the data generated by traffic on the website Iâ⊚⊚m monitoring with Google Analytics:

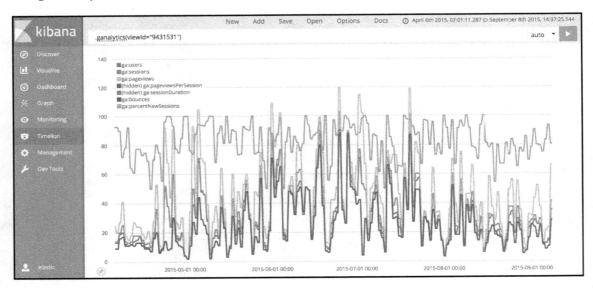

ganalytics expression results

The data can simply be verified from within the Google Analytics console, and can be updated as they are generated.

Our development environment is now ready. In the next section, we'll go through the implementation details of this extension.

Walking through the implementation

In this section, we'll focus on the implementation logic of the extension. We'll explore building and packaging in the next section. Let's first review the structure of the project:

```
$ ls -lrt
LICENSE
gulpfile.js
index.js
functions
mkdocs.yml
timelion-google-analytics.png
README.md
docs
package.json
node_modules
test.sh
```

We'll explain the role of each file throughout this chapter, but for implementation only the following files should be considered:

- `index.js`: To load our extension functions in Timelion
- `functions/ganalytics`: Contains the function implementation
- `functions/google_utils`: Contains the `helper` functions

google_utils.js

`index.js` is a mandatory file that, as explained, will inject the expression in the available Timelion functions. Its implementation is pretty straightforward, and you can reuse it across the extension you want to create:

```
module.exports = function (kibana) {
  return new kibana.Plugin({
    name: 'timelion-google-analytics',
    require: ['timelion'],
    init: function (server) {
      server.plugins.timelion.addFunction(
        require('./functions/ganalytics'));
    }
```

```
    });
  };
```

index.js directly references the ganalytics.js file, and calls the addFunction function to add it to the Timelion function library. You can have as many instances of addFunction as you have functions to load.

The google_utils.js file contains functions that are used by the ganalytics.js file, such as a function to authorize the user to connect to GARA:

```
module.exports.authorize = function(request, tlConfig) {
  return new Promise(function (resolve, reject) {
    var key = {...}
    var jwtClient = new google.auth.JWT(key.client_email, null,
    key.private_key,
      ["https://www.googleapis.com/auth/analytics"],null);
    jwtClient.authorize(function(err, tokens) {
      if (err) {
        reject(err);
      }
      resolve({
        'headers': {'Content-Type': 'application/json'},
        'auth': jwtClient,
        'resource': request,
      });
    });
  });
}
```

As you can see, the function uses the JSON key (I deliberately hid it here to shorten the code for the sake of readability), so that, if you check the source file, you will see I have populated the key using the timelion config object. Here is an example:

```
"type": tlConfig.settings['timelion:google.service_account.type']
```

The key is then used to build a JWT client (JSON Web Token—more info at https://jwt.io) to authorize Timelion to access GARA.

If authorized, the function will return an authorized JWT client, which can be used by other functions, such as the second function in the file:

```
module.exports.getReport = function(request) {
  return new Promise(function(resolve, reject) {
    analyticsreporting.reports.batchGet(request, function(err,
    resp) {
      var metricsList =
_.map(resp.reports[0].columnHeader.metricHeader.metricHeaderEntries,
```

```
        function(metric){
            return metric.name;
        });
        var data = resp.reports[0].data.rows;
        var lists = [];
        for ( var i=0, l=metricsList.length; i<l; i++ ) {
          var serieList = {
            data: [],
            type: 'series',
            label: metricsList[i]
          }
          serieList.data = _.map(data, function(item) {
            return [ moment(item.dimensions, "YYYYMMDD").format("x"),
              item.metrics[0].values[i] ]
          });
          lists.push(serieList);
        }
        resolve({
          type: 'seriesList',
          list: lists
        });
      });
    });
  }
```

The goal of the `getReport` function is to fetch the data from GARA and format it for Timelion. The final series list contains one series for each metric passed to the `.ganalytics` expression. For example, say you pass the following:

```
.ganalytics(viewId="9235382", metrics="user,sessions,bounces" )
```

The `getReport` will create three series and add them to the series list. As explained, the function formats the data. Say you try to display the content of the GARA response object like this:

```
console.log(resp.reports[0])
```

You should see something like this:

```
{ columnHeader:
   { dimensions: [ 'ga:date' ],
     metricHeader: { metricHeaderEntries: [Object] } },
  data:
   { rows: [ [Object] ],
     totals: [ [Object] ],
     rowCount: 1,
     minimums: [ [Object] ],
     maximums: [ [Object] ] } }
```

So the returned object is composed of a list of metrics (`metricHeaderEntries`): obviously the one we passed in the request, and also the corresponding list of values stored in the `rows` array. If we take a look at one item of this array, here is what we have:

```
{ dimensions: [ '20161014' ],
  metrics: [ { values: [ '23',
  '27',
  '51',
  '1.8888888888888888',
  '4359.0',
  '13',
  '70.37037037037037' ]
  } ] }
```

In the preceding example, the `dimensions` field contains the timestamp, metrics, and the related valuesâ⊚⊚in this case seven values because the request contained seven metrics, such as `users`, `session`, `bounces`. In any case, the preceding item needs to be formatted as follows:

```
[ timestamp, value ]
```

This is done by the rest of the function. The result is then passed to the main function in `ganalytics.js`.

ganalytics.js

The `ganalytics.js` function just orchestrates the following steps.

It gathers the arguments, the view identifier, the dimensions list, and the time frame composed of the `startDate` and `endDate`. It also contains the metrics list, which, by default, contains the following values:

```
var config = _.defaults(args.byName, {
    metrics: "users, sessions, pageviews, pageviewsPerSession,
        sessionDuration, bounces, percentNewSessions"
    });
```

This explains why we had seven values in an item by default in `google_utils.js`.

Once the argument is set, the request is created:

```
var req = {
    reportRequests: [{
        viewId: viewId,
        dateRanges: [{
```

```
        startDate: startDate,
        endDate: endDate,
      }],
      metrics: _.map(metricsList, function(metric) {
        return { expression: metric }
      }),
      dimensions: _.map(dimensionsList, function(metric) {
        return { name: metric }
      })
    }]
  };
```

Then the process of authentication and data-fetching starts:

```
return googleUtils.authorize(req, tlConfig).then( function(request)
  {
      return
      googleUtils.getReport(request).then(function(seriesList) {
        return seriesList;
      });
  }, function(err) {
      console.log(err)
});
```

That's pretty much all we need on the implementation side. As you have seen, I've put all the Google API calls in the `google_utils.js`, which means that I could potentially extend the scope of this extension and perhaps add another Google API there. If I did so, then I would add another `Javascript` file that does the same orchestration as `ganalytics.js`, but which calls a different `google_utils.js` function.

When you finish implementing the plugin, you need to think about the release management aspects. This is what we'll look at in the next section.

Plugin release management

Release management is a crucial feature of Kibana extensions, as a plugin might not work from Kibana release to release: the Kibana plugin API is not stable yet so the API could be subject to changes and therefore does not guarantee backward compatibility. So, you need to keep track of new Kibana releases and update your plugin accordingly. This means that your users should be able to easily find the proper extension version on your repository. To do that, we'll first start by tagging our code base.

Tagging our code base and creating a release

To identify a specific version of our code, we'll use the concept of tags in Git. To do so we need to tag our code base as follows:

```
git tag <tagname>
```

Remember that we want our extension version to be aligned with the Kibana version as well. That is why, at the time of writing this book, if you check my repository tag, you will see that I've tagged the code as **v5.0.0-beta1**:

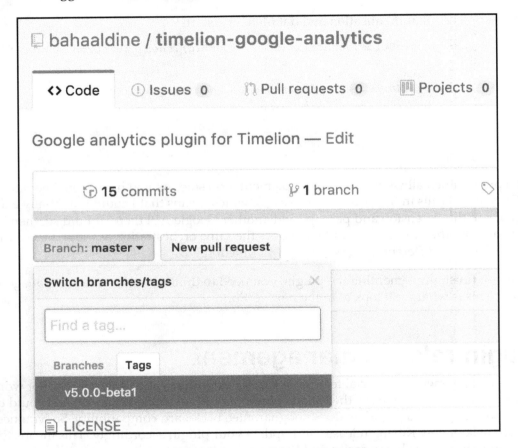

Timelion-google-analytics repository available tags

Tags are also essential in Github release management. If you try to create a release using tags (you can find a walkthrough of the steps for creating a release at `https://help.github.com/articles/creating-releases/`), you will get the following:

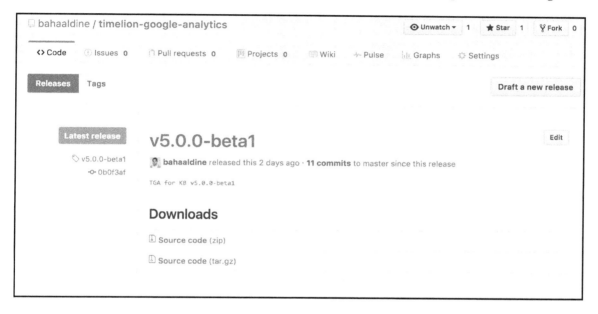

Creating a release from a tag

Now, with the releases in place, your users will be able to issue the following command to install the extension:

```
./bin/kibana-plugin install
https://github.com/bahaaldine/timelion-google-analytics/releases/download/v
ersion_name/timelion-google-5.0.0-beta1.zip
```

Summary

In this chapter, we have seen one way of customizing Kibana: extending the potential of Timelion by adding the ability to call Google Analytics Reporting API. In the next chapter, we'll go one step further and create a new Kibana plugin.

8
Anomaly Detection in Kibana 5.0

In September 2016, Elastic announced the acquisition of Prelert, now called Machine Learning, a behavioral analytics company. Prelert combines an anomaly detection engine, Elasticsearch for storing the analysis, and Kibana for visualizing the analysis.

The anomaly detection engine brings unsupervised machine learning capabilities to the Elastic Stack so that Prelert is able to learn from the data as it ingests them, and can highlight events that deviate from expectations.

In this chapter we'll explore the following:

- Applying the use case of Prelert to find a solution in anomaly detection
- Using Prelert and Kibana for operational analytics
- Leveraging Timelion, X-Pack alerting, and reporting features to visualize and be apprised of anomalies

 As a disclaimer, the version of Prelert used in this chapter is an exclusive preview of what Prelert will look like in the upcoming GA version. It's not a public version.
At the time of writing this chapter, the current public version that still runs on Kibana 4.0 is 2.1.2. This is the one to use to run your project.

Understanding the concept of anomaly detection

In this section, we'll try to summarize how Prelert solves the challenge of anomaly detection by first understanding why data visualization is a sufficient medium when it comes to pointing out an anomaly, and then we'll see why traditional alerting systems cannot be used at scale for anomaly detection.

Understanding human limits with regard to data visualization

Anomaly detection is the art of detecting things that shouldn't occur, or that differ from normal occurrences. Anomaly detection is the general name given to a statistical modeling technique used to identify unusual patterns in time-based events.

If we take the following dashboard, we can see different things happening:

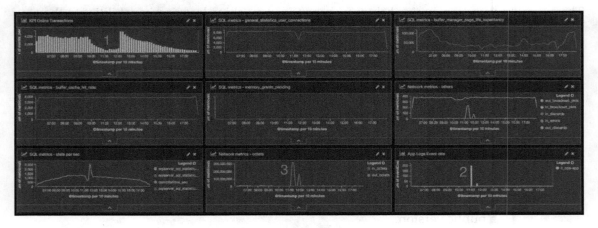

IT ops dashboard with potential anomalies

In the preceding screenshot, we can see a significant drop in the first graph (point 1). This looks suspicious, and may indicate a problem. Now, compared with the rest of the charts alongside it, we see that the increases in points **2** and **3** seem to be correlated in time with the previous drop. But all of these are only assumptions based on what our eye sees, and can be interpreted differently from one eye to another. Another issue is that sometimes anomalous events are not so easy to notice in a chart. The following chart illustrates this point:

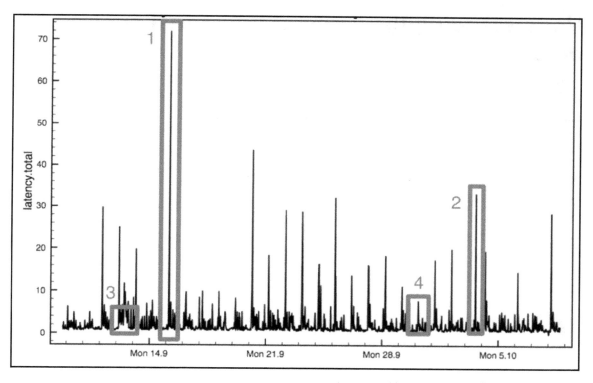

Time series data with nonobvious anomalies

Lets assume you are tasked with identifying usual activity in the above time series chart. You might identify a sharp increase in the event rate (**1**), and drop (**4**), but we can also see an abnormal base rate in the event rate over a given period of time (**2**). While your eye might be good at identifying subtle pattern changes, it would find it much harder to infer importance to chart point 3, where a significant increase happens in the chart. If we zoom in on this part, we'll notice that the increase is unexpected for this period of time, and that's the real anomaly.

So it is obvious from the preceding example that the events saturate the human eye, which thus gives a wrong sense of the data. Another issue caused by this is that, when it comes to alerts, you are not always watching your dashboard, and expect to get notified as soon as something unexpected happens.

In the next section, we shall see the usual strategy employed for this and its consequences.

Understanding the limits of traditional anomaly detection

When doing metric analytics on multiple network devices, for instance, you could end up with the following kinds of dashboard:

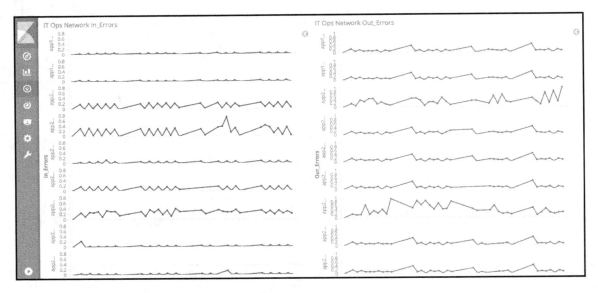

Network dashboard

The preceding screenshot has the same problem that we have seen earlier, namely it is very hard for a human to detect what the anomaly is in the data. Furthermore, if the strategy is to automate detection through alerts, the number of devices that are to be monitored for change is so high that we would end up building a considerable number of rules per device based on static thresholds, which might not be valid over time. As a result, we would need maintenance.

Another issue concerns simple statistic-oriented alerting. We could also fall into the trap of false positive and false negative alerts, as the following chart shows:

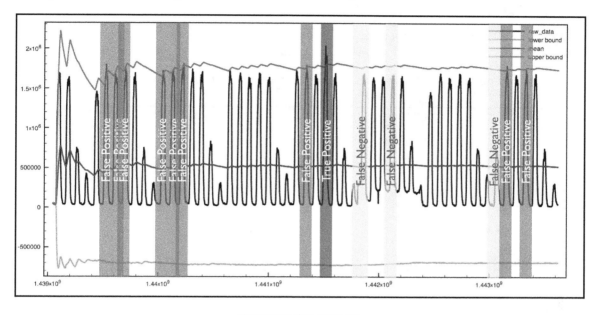

False positive and false negative alerts

This would effectively cancel all the benefits of alerting as the operator would receive a high number of alerts, many of which indicated normal operations.

This is where Prelert's approach comes in handy in solving anomaly detection through unsupervised machine learning.

Understanding how Prelert solves anomaly detection

Building on what was mentioned earlier, Prelert generates its results using unsupervised machine learning on top of periodic time series data. It effectively learns the following:

- The periodicity of the data, as shown in the following screenshot:

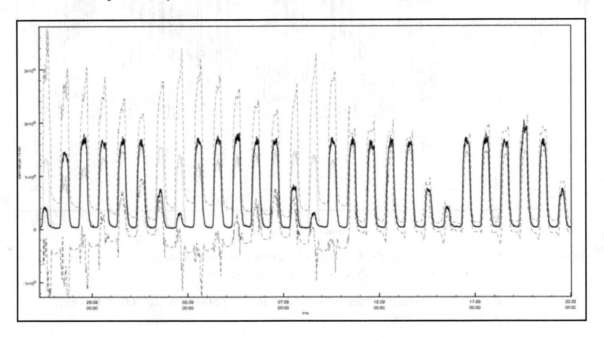

Periodicity trend learning

The solid black line represents the source data, the red dashed data is the upper bound of the calculated model, and the dark blue dashed line is the lower bound of the model. The teal line is the mean expected signal. As you can see, the source is periodic, and Prelert learns the periodicity of the model represented by the other lines getting closer and closer to the signal.

- It is possible to estimate how likely an event is to occur by calculating the probability density distribution, as the following screenshot shows:

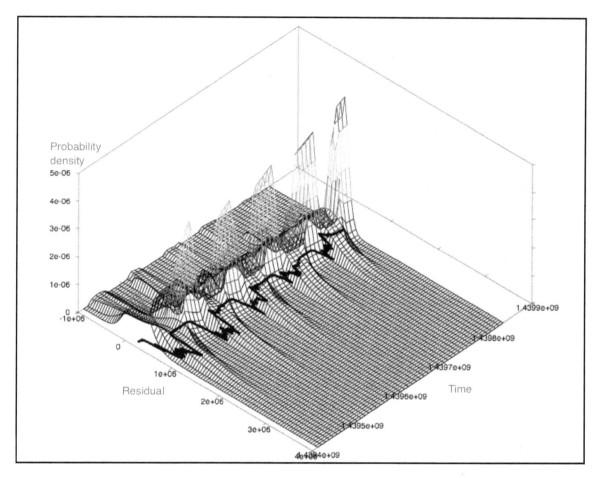

Probability density distribution

The preceding figure represents the probability density distribution over time for the residual of the signal (the blue line shown in the next diagram). The variance of the probability here is due to the scale being a function of time, which essentially means that Prelert can understand and account for the variance for different periods of the day (day versus night, for example).

- Detect how much an event deviates from the normal, as illustrated by the following screenshot:

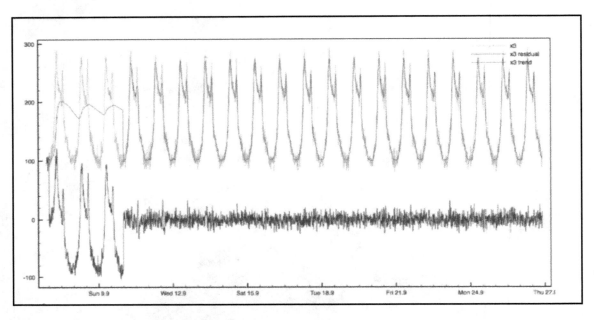

Residual when subtracting out the periodic trend

The preceding graph represents the residual (red line) when subtracting the periodic trend (blue line) from the signal (orange line). From this, Prelert knows directly whether or not an event should occur when the model is stable (in this case, after three periods).

- In the next section, we are going to use what we have learned in previous chapters to implement the operational analytics use case, bearing in mind the limits of traditional anomaly detection. We will also look at how Prelert solves the challenge of anomaly detection.

Using Prelert for operational analytics

In this section, we'll use what we learned in `Chapter 5`, *Metric Analytics with Metricbeat and Kibana 5.0* and apply it to Prelert. The idea is to use **Metricbeat** to generate system data and analyze the CPU utilization, as well as to detect anomalies. We'll run Metricbeat on our machines; you can do the same on a different machine, if you have some on Amazon, for instance. Wherever you do it, we'll also run a stress tool to generate CPU utilization, just to facilitate the demo so that we are sure that we have the anomalies.

The first thing to do is download Metricbeat, install it, and import Kibana dashboards, as shown in `Chapter 5`, *Metric Analytics with Metricbeat and Kibana 5.0*; refer to this chapter for more details. Once installed, run Metricbeat and start generating data.

Setting up Prelert

At the time of writing, only four weeks have passed since Prelert was acquired by Elastic, which means that the integration of Prelert in Elastic Stack is still ongoing. Therefore, you'll see two aspects of Prelert here:

- On your side, you will download and use the current version that uses Kibana 4.
- On my side, I'll show you screenshots of Prelert integration in Kibana 5, which is, again, not GA yet, at the time of writing. It should only be considered as a preview that gives a sense of what things will look like when integration is complete.

That being established, let's start setting up Prelert on your machine. First download the current version from
`http://www.prelert.com/reg/behavioral-analytics-elastic-trial.html`.

You will see that you need to register in order to download Prelert. Please do so and then proceed to download. The Prelert installer contains everything you need. Execute the installer as follows:

```
$ chmod +x prelert_engine_2.1.2_release_macosx_64bit.bin
$ ./prelert_engine_2.1.2_release_macosx_64bit.bin
```

The Prelert installer will start, and you will be asked the following questions, to which you can give the answers in bold. When no answers are given, the default will be used:

```
Do you wish to continue? [N]: Y
Please enter the license key provided by Prelert []: the license
key you received by email
```

```
Please enter the top level Prelert Engine installation directory
[/opt/prelert/prelert_home]:
/Users/bahaaldine/Downloads/prelert_pack_home
'/Users/bahaaldine/Downloads/prelert_pack_home' does not exist -
would you like to create it now? [Y]: Y
Would you like to configure advanced options? [N]: Y
Please enter the Prelert Engine data directory
[/Users/bahaaldine/Downloads/prelert_pack_home/cots/elasticsearch/data
  ]:
'/Users/bahaaldine/Downloads/prelert_pack_home/cots/elasticsearch/data'
does not exist - would you like to create it now? [Y]: Y
Please enter the Prelert Engine logs directory
[/Users/bahaaldine/Downloads/prelert_pack_home/logs]:
'/Users/bahaaldine/Downloads/prelert_pack_home/logs' does not exist -
  would you like to create it now? [Y]: Y
```

The Prelert installer will check whether the ports used by the Elasticsearch instance, the engine, and Kibana are already used by other processes. Because you should have your Elastic Stack 5.0 running on your machine, the port should already be used, as the following logs show:

```
Elasticsearch HTTP port                    9200 NOT AVAILABLE
Elasticsearch transport port range start   9300 NOT AVAILABLE
Elasticsearch transport port range end     9400 Available
Kibana HTTP port                           5601 NOT AVAILABLE
Prelert Engine REST API HTTP port          8080 NOT AVAILABLE
```

You will just need to set the available ports:

```
Elasticsearch HTTP port [9200]: 9201
Elasticsearch transport port range start [9300]: 9500
Elasticsearch transport port range end [9400]: 9600
Kibana HTTP port [5601]: 5701
Prelert Engine REST API HTTP port [8080]: 8081
```

The checks should be fine:

```
Elasticsearch HTTP port                    9201 Available
Elasticsearch transport port range start   9500 Available
Elasticsearch transport port range end     9600 Available
Kibana HTTP port                           5701 Available
Prelert Engine REST API HTTP port          8081 Available
Are the TCP ports that Prelert Engine is going to use acceptable to
  you? [Y]:Y
```

At the end of the installation, just proceed to the Prelert launch:

```
Would you like to start the Prelert Engine now? [Y]:
```

Once the startup is complete, you should get the following kinds of message (depending on the port you set):

```
The Prelert Engine REST API is available at http://MacBook-Pro-de-
    Bahaaldine.local:8081/engine/v2
The Prelert Engine Dashboard is available at http://MacBook-Pro-de-
    Bahaaldine.local:5701/app/prelert
To access the Prelert Engine REST API remotely, ensure TCP port 8081 is
    not blocked
by any firewall, and then point a web browser at one of:
http://192.168.0.16:8081/engine/v2
http://MacBook-Pro-de-Bahaaldine.local:8081/engine/v2
(depending on whether DNS is available)
```

Then, if you try to browse to `http://localhost:8081` (adapt the port based on your configuration), you should get the following simple page, which contains the link to the engine API and the link to the dashboard:

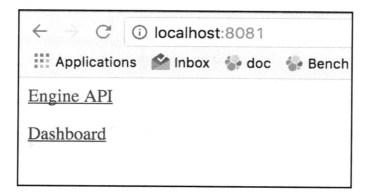

Prelert main page

Click on both links to check that everything was installed correctly:

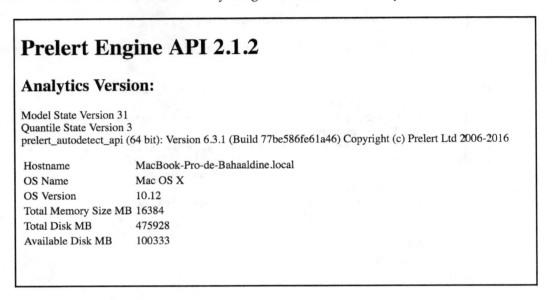

Information after clicking on the engine API link

The above image gives information about the installed Prelert version and host information. We are now ready to create the Prelert job on top of our Metricbeat data.

Clicking on Dashboard will bring you to the Prelert console where the job creation takes place:

Prelert in Kibana

Creating a Prelert job

In this section, even if we are not running the exact same version of Prelert, job creation will still look the same, so there won't be differences in the screenshots.

A Prelert Job is a unit that executes a plan a user configures in the Prelert console. The job plan configuration consists of going through a wizard where the user can model the KPI on which he wants to apply anomaly detection.

There are two options to create a Prelert job: you can either create it manually in Kibana, or through the Prelert API. We'll use the first option, and I'll point out the place where you will find a JSON example in case you want to use the REST API.

To start creating a job, connect to the Prelert Kibana dashboard at `http://localhost:5701/app/prelert` and start creating a job by hitting the Create new job button:

Create a new job

Choose a data source

Elasticsearch server
Specify the address of an Elasticsearch server.

File upload
Upload a file containing a data set. Maximum size is 100MB.

Other data source
Create a job without reference to source data. Specify fields manually and upload data later using the API.

First step when creating a Prelert job: Choose a data source

Prelert gives you the possibility of grabbing the data from Elasticsearch, from a CSV file or even from a different REST API. In our case, we'll select the first choice, namely an Elasticsearch index:

Configure the Elasticsearch data source

In the preceding image, I am just passing all the information to connect to Elasticsearch (I am using an instance without X-Pack security here, but if you choose to use one with X-Pack security, tick the authenticated checkbox and enter your credentials), and I pick the indices from which I want to pull the data (`metricbeat*`).

The index contains different types, but here I just want to work with the **metricsets** type, and finally use the `@timestamp` field as a timefield. Click on **Next**, and you will get the following wizard with different subsections:

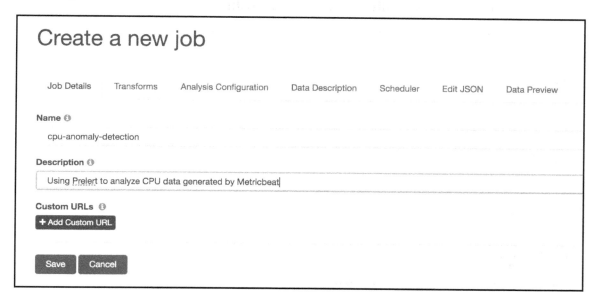

Job creation options

The preceding screenshot shows the different steps you can go through to create a job:

- **Job details**: Here you can give a name and a description to your job.
- **Transforms**: Here you can configure data transformation options. We won't use that section as the data are already formatted in the proper way when they are collected by Metricbeat.

Analysis configuration is the main section in job creation as this is where anomaly detection is actually configured. This section has a multitude of settings, which are all documented, and for the sake of simplicity, in this chapter I'm only going to focus on the notion of detection.

If you click on the **Add Detector** button, you will be able to add a new detector that will analyze the incoming data based on a function that you can pick for it. Prelert has a number of built-in functions to choose from; in our case, we will create a detector that uses the `metric` function, which essentially analyzes the data with `mean`, `min`, and `max` functions:

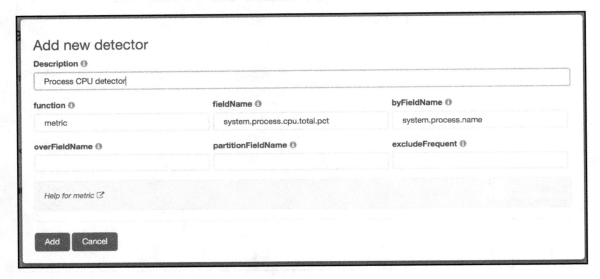

Adding a new CPU process detector

The preceding detector also uses the `system.process.name` to break down the analysis per process:

- **Data description** allows you to set the time field and the pattern to describe the data format.
- **Scheduler** is where you can set how the Prelert scheduler will ingest the data. Prelert uses a scan and scroll API to grab the data per batch. So, for example, here you can set the frequency at which the data are scrolled or the scroll size itself:

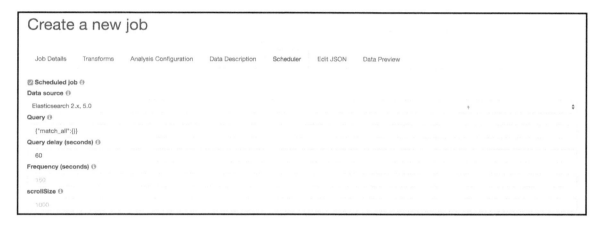

Scheduler configuration

- **Edit JSON**: Contains the JSON configuration for the job we are creating. It's actually the JSON that you can use as an input of the job creation Prelert REST API.
- **Data preview**: Gives a preview of what the scheduler will ingest.

Once the detector is created, click on the **Save** button to create the job. A popup will point out that no influencers have been created: We don't need one, we don't expect any other data in our document to influence the anomaly detection. Then the scheduler will show a popup to configure from when the data should be ingested, as shown here:

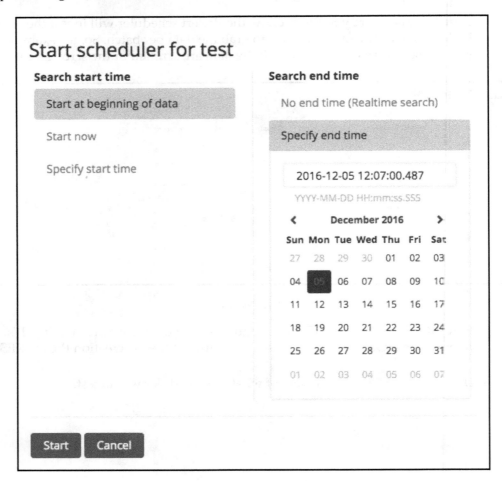

Start time configuration

In our case, we'll start from the beginning of the data to the oldest time period in the data set, so that Prelert will have historical data to start building its anomaly detection model. If you click on **Start**, the job will start scrolling the data, and you should see it pulling data from your Metricbeat index:

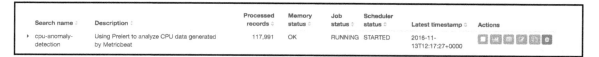

Search name	Description	Processed records	Memory status	Job status	Scheduler status	Latest timestamp	Actions
▸ cpu-anomaly-detection	Using Prelert to analyze CPU data generated by Metricbeat	117,991	OK	RUNNING	STARTED	2016-11-13T12:17:27+0000	

Created job pulling the data

While Prelert is analyzing the data, you can access the dashboard to see whether there are anomalies detected yet by clicking on the **Open results** button:

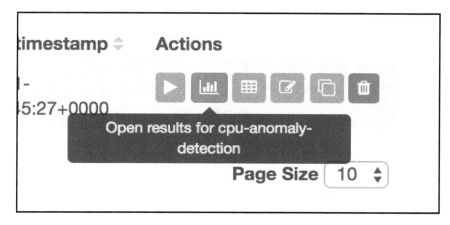

Available actions button for each Prelert job

The summary view shows an example of the source data on top and the different swim lanes chart containing identified anomalies in the signal:

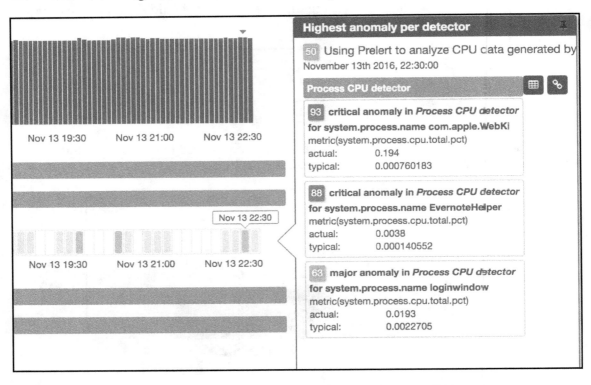

Summary view of Prelert in Kibana

As you see, there are some critical anomalies that have been identified so far. Here, com.apple. Webkit seems to use more CPU (19%) than expected (0.07 percent) at the scale of the data. If I click on the Open explorer button, I will see the following:

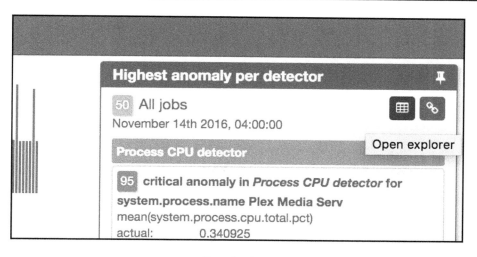

Open explorer button

To prove my point, I'll give more results of this type so that it is abundantly clear:

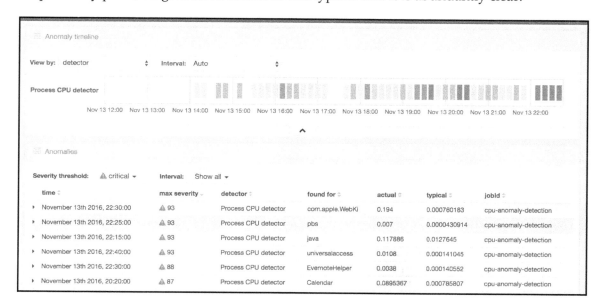

Open explorer view

I can filter each anomaly listed here by severity (the preceding image only shows critical anomalies). You also have the option of expanding the details.

⊞ Anomalies

Severity threshold: ⚠ critical ▾   **Interval:** Show all ▾

time ⇕	max severity ⌄	detector ⇕
▼ November 13th 2016, 22:30:00	⚠ 93	Process CPU detector

Description:
critical anomaly in Process CPU detector found for system.process.name com.apple.WebKi

Anomaly Details:

system.process.name:	com.apple.WebKi ⊕ ⊖
time:	November 13th 2016, 22:30:00 to November 13th 2016, 22:35:00
function:	metric
fieldName:	system.process.cpu.total.pct
actual:	0.194
typical:	0.000760183
job ID:	cpu-anomaly-detection ⊕ ⊖
probability:	1.47031e-21

Anomaly details

For the CPU anomaly caused by the **com.appleWebkit** process, the score is pretty high (93) because it is directly proportional to the very low likelihood of this event (**1.47031e-21**).

One word about our data

There might not be enough of it for Prelert to build an accurate model. At least in my case, the anomaly could start to be relevant after 1 week of using my laptop normally. For it to be really relevant, I recommend running this in a more intensive utilization environment, and for a longer period.

To show you a preview of what the Prelert 5.x user interface will look like, I'm not going to use our dataset, but a different one where the periodic trend of the data is clearly visible:

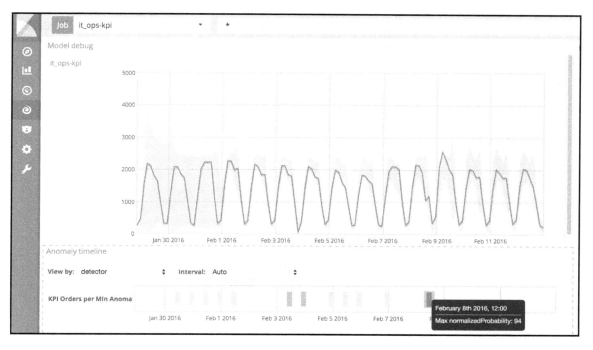

Prelert preview in Kibana 5.0

In the preceding image, the blue line represents the signal, whereas the blue area represents the model built by Prelert. At the beginning of the chart, the model is not even close to the data, but the more we go forward in time, the more the model narrows down towards the signal.

In the preceding example, at some point an anomaly is detected (with a score of 94) when an unusual drop happens in the signal data. On the other hand, if I open explorer with our Metricbeat data, here is what I get:

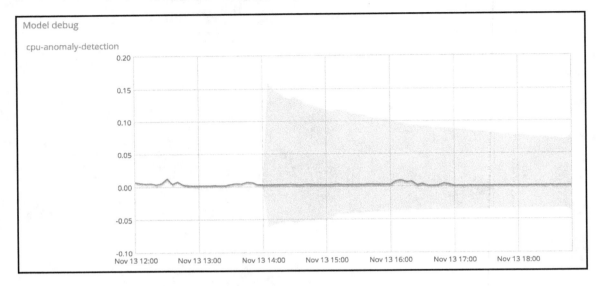

Model very far from the reality

Again, because we are working with very short-term data without too much historical data for Prelert, the model will get more and more accurate over time.

Now that we have an anomaly detection job running, how about combining the result with the alert functionality in order to enable reporting in Kibana 5.0? This is what we are going to see in the next section.

Combining Prelert, alerting, and Timelion

Prelert detects anomalies in data indexed in Elasticsearch, stores its results in Elasticsearch, but also provides out of the box dashboards to explore and understand anomalies. The Elastic stack provides a holistic platform for data analysis, in which we can just pick products to extend our anomaly detection experience. X-Pack alerting is the first choice as it could consume Prelert results to trigger relevant and accurate alerts. Timelion is also a fantastic choice to correlate the anomaly detection result to source data by using the statistics functions and customization features that it offers.

As said earlier, Prelert exposes a REST API that allows you to manage a job and get the result of the analysis.

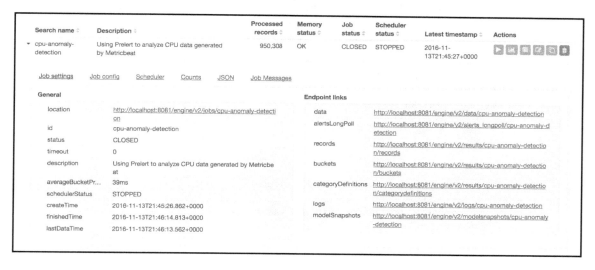

Job details and endpoints

The preceding image details an **Endpoint links** section in which the REST APIs that we are going to use for alerting are listed. All APIs are documented at `http://www.prelert.com/docs/products/latest/engine_api_reference/results/result s.html`. We will use the generic Record API endpoint for our discussion, which returns anomaly detect on results.

Visualizing anomaly results in Timelion

Timelion is great way to visualize time series data. As seen in `Chapter 5`, *Metric Analytics with Metricbeat and Kibana 5.0*, we will leverage its feature in this section in order to visualize the result of anomaly detection and draw a customized visualization.

Because the Prelert installation lives on its own Elasticsearch cluster, the first thing we need is to ingest data created by Prelert to bring them into the Kibana 5.0 Elasticsearch cluster. To do so, I have prepared a small Python script that you will find in the attached chapter source at `https://github.com/bahaaldine/packt-kibana-5.0`.

If you call the record API, in my case, `http://localhost:8081/engine/v2/results/cpu-anomaly-detection/records`, you will get the following record API output (remember that we have used the record endpoint for the sake of discussion):

```
{
   "hitCount" : 1193,
   "skip" : 0,
   "take" : 100,
   "nextPage" : "http://localhost:8081/engine/v2/results/cpu-anomaly-
      detection/records/?
   skip=100&take=100&includeInterim=false&sort=normalizedProbability
      &desc=true&anomalyScore=0%2C0&normalizedProbability=0%2C0",
   "previousPage" : null,
   "documents" : [ {
      "timestamp" : "2016-11-14T03:20:00.000+0000",
      "bucketSpan" : 300,
      "fieldName" : "system.process.cpu.total.pct",
      "function" : "mean",
      "normalizedProbability" : 95.71811,
      "anomalyScore" : 50.5083,
      "detectorIndex" : 0,
      "initialNormalizedProbability" : 96.9458,
      "byFieldValue" : "Plex Media Serv",
      "functionDescription" : "mean",
      "typical" : 6.70872E-4,
      "actual" : 0.340925,
      "probability" : 9.75444E-44,
      "byFieldName" : "system.process.name",
      "isInterim" : false
   }
...
```

The Python script keeps calling the API till the nextPage field has a value and, for each batch of 100 records, calls the Elasticsearch bulk API, using the Elasticsearch Python API (`https://www.elastic.co/guide/en/elasticsearch/client/python-api/current/index.html`):

```
for record in response.json()['documents']:
action = {
   "_index": "prelert",
   "_type": "record",
```

```
    "_source": record
  }
  actions.append(action)

  if len(actions) > 0:
  helpers.bulk(es, actions)
```

To call the script, run the following command:

```
./grab_prelert_results.py URL_TO_THE_RECORD_API
```

Just replace the argument with your record API URL, then connect to the Kibana 5.0 dev tools, and you should get a cpu-anomaly-detection-results index created with the `record` documents:

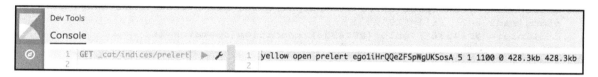

Checking if the cpu-anomaly-detection-results index has been created properly

Now, with Timelion, we'll create a visualization that shows the following:

- The signal, namely, the maximum CPU usage on the machine over time
- The different levels of anomalies (in other words, warning, minor, major, and critical anomalies)

To do so, we'll leverage the variable feature in Timelion, which allows storing expressions. This variable feature can be directly used in the expression bar.

We will create five different: four for the anomaly level, one for the data source:

```
# Warning level
$warning=.es(index=cpu-anomaly-detection-results,
timefield=timestamp).divide(.es(index=cpu-anomaly-detection-results,
timefield=timestamp)).multiply(.es(index=metricbeat*,
metric=max:system.process.cpu.total.pct).fit(mode=average).multiply(100)).p
oints(radius=3, fill="10",
fillColor="#2196F3").color(#2196F3).condition(operator=gt,
10).label(warning)
# Minor level
$minor=.es(index=cpu-anomaly-detection-results,
timefield=timestamp).divide(.es(index=cpu-anomaly-detection-results,
timefield=timestamp)).multiply(.es(index=metricbeat*,
metric=max:system.process.cpu.total.pct).fit(mode=average).multiply(100)).p
```

```
oints(radius=3, fill="10",
fillColor="#FFEB3B").color(#FFEB3B).condition(operator=lt,
10).condition(operator=gt, 50).label(minor)
# Major level
$major=.es(index=cpu-anomaly-detection-results,
timefield=timestamp).divide(.es(index=cpu-anomaly-detection-results,
timefield=timestamp)).multiply(.es(index=metricbeat*,
metric=max:system.process.cpu.total.pct).fit(mode=average).multiply(100)).p
oints(radius=3, fill="10",
fillColor="#FF9800").color(#FF9800).condition(operator=lt,
50).condition(operator=gt, 70).label(major)
# Critical level
$critical=.es(index=cpu-anomaly-detection-results,
timefield=timestamp).divide(.es(index=cpu-anomaly-detection-results,
timefield=timestamp)).multiply(.es(index=metricbeat*,
metric=max:system.process.cpu.total.pct).fit(mode=average).multiply(100)).p
oints(radius=3, fill="10",
fillColor="#F44336").color(#F44336).condition(operator=lt,
70).label(critical)
# Source signal
$maxCPU=.es(index=metricbeat*,
metric=max:system.process.cpu.total.pct).color(#00C853).fit(mode=averag
e).multiply(100).label("max cpu over time").bars(width=2)
# Render data
$maxCPU, $warning, $minor, $major, $critical
```

For the anomaly level, we are using the same normalization process that was mentioned in Chapter 5, *Metric Analytics with Metricbeat and Kibana 5.0,* by dividing the series list by itself and multiplying the result by the signal data so that the anomaly points are aligned with the source and precisely point to where the anomaly occurred.

The source signal is also the same as in Chapter 5, *Metric Analytics with Metricbeat and Kibana 5.0*: the maximum CPU used over time. If you copy and paste this expression in Timelion, here is what you will get:

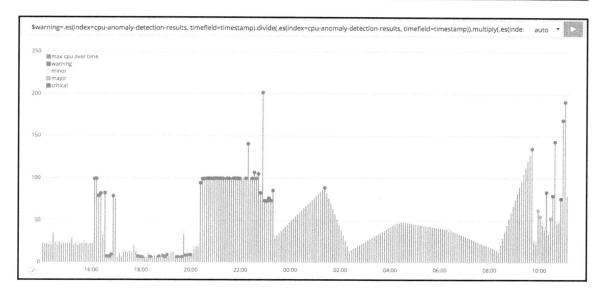

$warning=.es(index=cpu-anomaly-detection-results, timefield=timestamp).divide(.es(index=cpu-anomaly-detection-results, timefield=timestamp)).multiply(.es(inde:

Timelion anomaly detection chart

The signal represented by the green bar chart is decorated with points that display all levels of anomalies: Blue is **warning**, yellow is **minor**, orange is **major**, and red is **critical**. This provides a highly customizable way to visualize when anomalies have been detected over time, using both the anomaly records and the raw data. But we are not yet done. How about trying to associate a process name to an anomaly? It's completely feasible as Timelion charts can be saved as Kibana panels. Click the **Save** button, save the chart, create a new Kibana dashboard, and add the new panel

Save entire Timelion sheet

You want this option if you mostly use Timelion expressions from within the Timelion app and don't need to add Timelion charts to Kibana dashboards. You may also want this if you make use of references to other panels.

Save current expression as Kibana dashboard panel

Need to add a chart to a Kibana dashboard? We can do that! This option will save your currently selected expression as a panel that can be added to Kibana dashboards as you would add anything else. Note, if you use references to other panels you will need to remove the refences by copying the referenced expression directly into the expression you are saving. Click a chart to select a different expression to save.

Save expression as Kibana panel

So, to get the process name, we'll simply create a new Kibana visualization, a data table, that shows the top 20 processes with the highest CPU utilization:

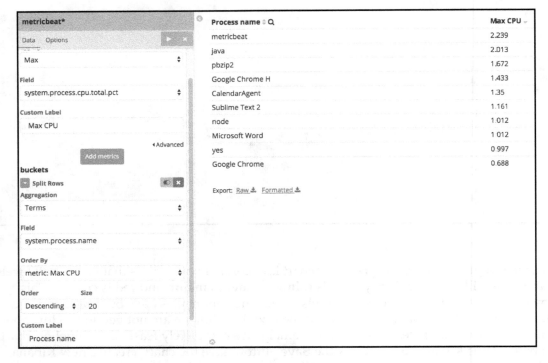

Data table creation

Save the data table. As you can see, the max CPU percentage is presented as a decimal, but Kibana supports the customization of the data format. Go into the **management/index-patterns** section and look for the `system.process.cpu.total.pct` field in the `metricbeat*` index pattern:

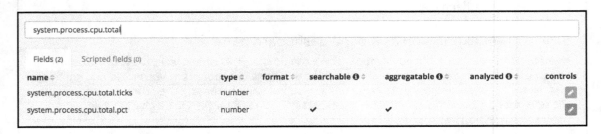

Kibana index-patterns field settings

Click on the **controls** button for the `system.process.cpu.total.pct` field and change the field format from default to Percentage:

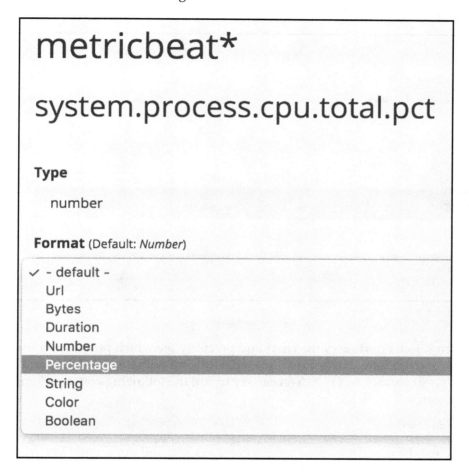

Changing field format from default to percentage

Leave the default settings as they are and update the field. Go back into the newly created dashboard and add the data table. You should get the following dashboard with the field formatted to percentage:

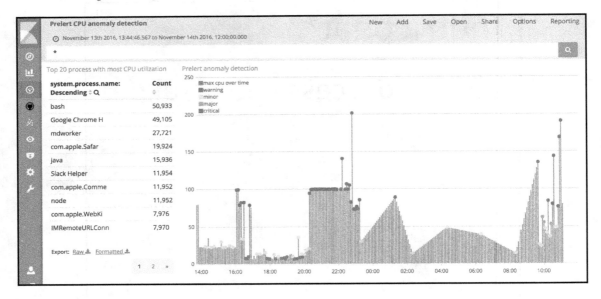

Prelert anomaly detection dashboard

Now you can select a portion of the chart and precisely see which processes consume the most CPU at a given time. In my case, I played a little bit with the `yes` command line, which essentially is a stress tool on OS X. You can try to run the following command and see that the CPU increases:

```
yes > /dev/null
```

I have launched the command at a random point in time, and apparently Prelert did the job of detecting something unusual happening:

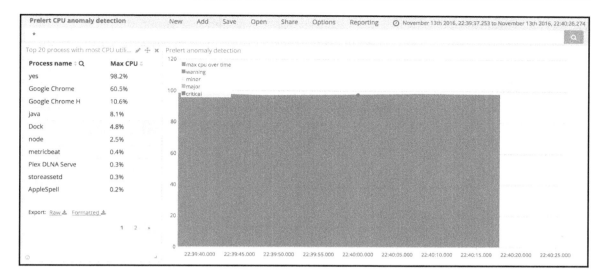

Identifying abnormal CPU consumption

Play with the dashboard, and try to identify which process was consuming your CPU based on the anomaly spots.

In real life, this dashboard might typically be browsed when a problem occurs, or sporadically throughout the day. Proactively being notified based on the anomaly score, or at least receiving a regular report on the situation, seems to be a better and more realistic option.

Scheduling anomaly detection reports with Reporting

In Kibana 5.0 the user is now able to export the dashboard to the PDF format manually through the **Reporting** button or in the dashboard itself:

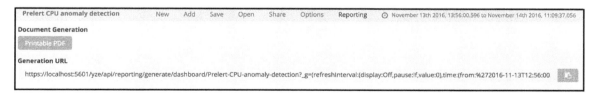

Generate a new report

When the **Printable PDF** button is clicked, the report is added to a generation queue, which can be accessed under the **Management/Reporting** section, from where the report can be downloaded:

Management / **Kibana**

Index Patterns   **Saved Objects**   **Reporting**   **Advanced Settings**

Generated Reports

Filter Reports: ☑ **Only show my reports**

Document	**Added**
Prelert CPU anomaly detection dashboard	2016-11-14 @ 5:09 PM elastic
Prelert CPU anomaly detection dashboard	2016-11-14 @ 3:05 PM elastic

Report generation queue

The other way to generate a report is to use the URL, which is given when you click on the **Reporting** button in the dashboard. The following is an example of such a URL:

```
https://localhost:5601/yze/api/reporting/generate/dashboard/Prelert-CPU
-anomaly-
detection?_g=(refreshInterval:(display:Off,pause:!f,value:0),time:(from
:%272016-11-13T12:56:00.596Z%27,interval:auto,mode:absolute,timezone:Eu
rope%2FBerlin,to:%272016-11-14T10:09:37.056Z%27))&_a=(filters:!(),optio
ns:(darkTheme:!f),panels:!((col:1,id:Prelert-warning-
anomalies,panelIndex:3,row:1,size_x:3,size_y:2,type:visualization),(col
:4,id:Prelert-minor-
anomalies,panelIndex:4,row:1,size_x:3,size_y:2,type:visualization),(col
:7,id:Prelert-major-
anomalies,panelIndex:5,row:1,size_x:3,size_y:2,type:visualization),(col
:10,id:Prelert-critical-
anomalies,panelIndex:6,row:1,size_x:3,size_y:2,type:visualization),(col
:1,id:Top-20-process-with-most-CPU-
utilization,panelIndex:1,row:3,size_x:3,size_y:5,type:visualization),(c
ol:4,id:Prelert-anomaly-
```

```
detection,panelIndex:2,row:3,size_x:9,size_y:5,type:visualization)),que
ry:(query_string:(analyze_wildcard:!t,query:%27*%27)),title:%27Prelert+
CPU+anomaly+detection%27,uiState:(P-1:(vis:(params:(sort:(columnIndex:!
n,direction:!n))))))&sync
```

This can be reduced manually to its shortest recommended form:

```
https://localhost:5601/yze/api/reporting/generate/dashboard/Prelert-CPU
-anomaly-detection?sync.
```

Note that the `sync` parameter is mandatory to generate the PDF. From there, we can combine alerting and reporting to schedule daily reports. You first need to add some configuration to your `elasticsearch.yml` file, to access your email server as described in the documentation found at
`https://www.elastic.co/guide/en/x-pack/current/actions-email.html#configuring-e mail`.

Then, from the Kibana dev tools, issue the following command to create the alert:

```
PUT /_xpack/watcher/watch/cpu_anomaly_detection_report?pretty
{
  "trigger": {
    "schedule": {
      "interval": "1d"
    }
  },
  "actions": {
    "send_email": {
      "email": {
        "to": "recipient@email.com",
        "subject": "CPU anomalies daily report",
        "body": "Please find attached the report",
        "attachments": {
          "cpu_anomalies.pdf": {
            "http": {
              "content_type": "application/pdf",
              "request": {
                "method": "POST",
                "headers": {
                  "kbn-xsrf": "reporting"
                },
                "auth": {
                  "basic": {
                    "username": "elastic_username",
                    "password": "elastic_password"
                  }
                },
                "read_timeout": "300s",
```

```
                    "url":
"https://localhost:5601/yze/api/reporting/generate/dashboard/Prelert-CPU-an
omaly-detection?sync"
                        }
                    }
                }
            }
        }
    }
}
```

The preceding command uses a simple scheduler to trigger the alert every day. Then an action is taken, in this case, the sending of an e-mail with a PDF attached to it. We use the URL given by Kibana to generate the report, and our credentials to call the API. Once the alert is created, you should start seeing history documents being created in the `.watcher-history*` index; you should also get an anomaly detection PDF every day in your inbox.

Summary

In this chapter, we have seen why traditional approaches to anomy detection quickly converge to their limit, whether from a human point of view (because of the amount of information to digest); or from the technical point of view where traditional statistical methodologies generate false positives or true negatives. Then we leverage the dataset and use cases build in the previous chapter to illustrate how Kibana can be used for anomaly detection based on the unsupervised machine learning feature that Machine Learning brings to the Elastic Stack.

In the next and final chapters, we'll tackle the subject of Kibana custom plugin creation by first setting up the development environment and then implementing the plugin.

9
Creating a Custom Plugin for Kibana 5.0

Earlier in this book, we looked at how to extend an existing Kibana plugin, namely, Timelion. We also tried to extend the visualization palette and add our own visualizations to Kibana dashboards.

Now, in this final chapter, we'll learn how to leverage the stack-management architecture Kibana provides to extend the existing capabilities through the creation of a new plugin.

To be a bit more specific, we will be covering the following topics in this chapter:

- Developing a plugin and looking at how to set up the environment to develop a plugin, which is similar to what we did with Timelion, with the difference of code structure
- Once we have our environment ready, we'll dig into the implementation of a topology explorer plugin, which will allow you to visualize your Elasticsearch cluster topology

Creating a plugin from scratch

When I say from scratch, it's not totally accurate, as we are going to use a plugin generator made by the Kibana team itself.

In this section, we'll first start to use **Yeoman** to generate a plugin and analyze its structure.

Yeoman – the plugin scaffolder

It's not obvious to start developing a Kibana, specifically when you don't know what the project structure looks like, what are the required dependencies, or how to build it. This is where Yeoman will you get started.

 Yeoman is a utility tool to scaffold new projects such as a Kibana plugin.

You can access more documentation from `http://yeoman.io/` and specifically on the generator discovery section, `http://yeoman.io/generators/`, which allows searching for Yeoman generators:

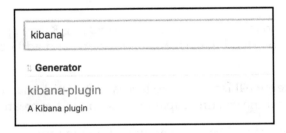

Yeoman generator discovery

Yeoman needs to be installed using Node.js in order to be used; you just need to issue the following command:

```
npm install -g yo
```

We will also install the Kibana plugin generator, the code for which can be found at the following link: `https://github.com/elastic/generator-kibana-plugin`

The installation command line is as follows:

```
npm install -g yo generator-kibana-plugin
```

Once Yeoman and the generator are installed, create a folder where your Kibana plugin will be stored and issue the following command to generate the plugin:

```
yo kibana-plugin
```

This will launch a wizard that will ask you the following questions; I've put my answers in bold:

```
? Your Plugin Name topology
? Short Description a cluster topology explorer plugin
? Target Kibana Version 5.0.0
```

The generator will create a generic code template and install the minimal dependencies to use the plugin. Listing the files in the newly generated plugin should give you the following output:

```
$ ls -l
README.md
index.js
node_modules
package.json
public
server
```

In Chapter 7, *Customizing Kibana 5.0 Timelion*, we went through the description of each part of the Kibana plugin, so feel free to refer to that chapter for more clarification. What is important here is the fact that we are going to implement both server-side code that grabs data from the Elasticsearch REST API, and frontend code that will be stored in the public folder and will essentially use the server-side API to render a page.

Generating a **bare** plugin is pretty easy; you just need to follow the instructions, also in Chapter 7, *Customizing Kibana 5.0 Timelion*, regarding how to set up your environment for Kibana development. The only difference here is that the Gulp file to build and synchronize the plugin to Kibana is not provided in the generated plugin. The point is that we want to use the same synchronization mechanism that syncs all changes made during the development of our plugin to the Kibana installation folder.

That is why you have to create your own build configuration file; I've put an example in the chapter resources, which will hopefully help you with its creation: https://github.com/bahaaldine/packt-kibana-5.0/blob/master/chapter9/topology/gulpfile.js.

If you use this file to sync your plugin, remember to change the path to the Kibana installation directory, accessible at https://github.com/bahaaldine/packt-kibana-5.0/blob/master/chapter9/topology/gulpfile.js#L22.

The following path is what you will find in the plugin code, which corresponds to my environment:

```
dvar kibanaPluginDir = path.resolve(__dirname,
'/Users/bahaaldine/Dropbox/elastic/plugins/kibana/kibana5.0.0/plugins/' +
pkg.name);
```

Verifying our installation

We now need to verify whether the empty plugin structure we generated and our build configuration are working properly. We can verify the installation by using the following steps:

With the plugin generated, the Gulp file copied in the plugin directory, and the path to the Kibana installation directory changed, we'll now sync the plugin, as in Chapter 7, *Customizing Kibana 5.0 Timelion*, by first starting Kibana:

npm start

Type the following to sync the plugin:

gulp sync

Finally, by launching gulp in developer mode, all changes will be synced automatically:

gulp dev

At this point, if you launch Kibana with your freshly generated plugin, you should see a new topology plugin in the sidebar. Open it to get to the following landing page:

The preceding screenshot displays a landing page, which is generated based on the default template provided by a new plugin, stored in the following `public/templats/index.html` file:

```
<div class="container" ng-controller="testHelloWorld">
<div class="row">
<div class="col-12-sm">
<div class="well">
<h2>Congratulations</h2>
<p class="lead">You've successfully created your first Kibana Plugin!</p>
</div>
<h1>{{ title }}</h1>
<p class="lead">{{ description }}</p>
<p>The current time is {{ currentTime }}</p>
</div>
</div>
</div>
```

At this point, all aspects of your environment are ready to start implementing our topology plugin. In the next section, I'll walk you through the implementation of the plugin by describing the main parts of it.

A plugin to render Elasticsearch topology

The plugin I propose to create in this chapter will provide a way to get a better understanding of the cluster topology and, more specifically, how the data is distributed over indices, shards, and even down to the segment.

Topology will leverage an open source visualization framework. It is provided by *Baidu: ECharts 3*, which can be accessed at `http://echarts.baidu.com`. This visualization framework provides a very large palette of visualizations, and in particular one that is pretty handy to visualize data in clusters: the treemap visualization:

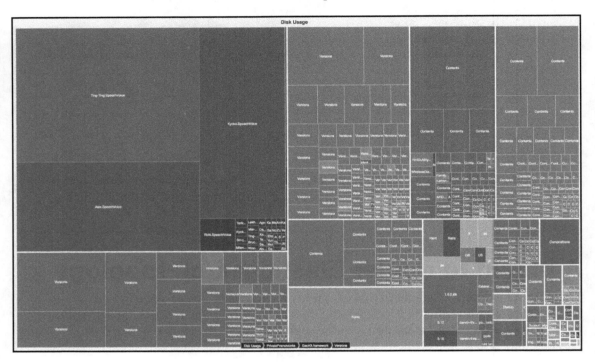

Treemap visualization displays data in clusters

The preceding example can be found here:
`http://echarts.baidu.com/demo.html#treemap-disk`.

As you can see, the data is organized in the form of multi-level clusters: if you click on one of them, you will drill down to the underlying level, and so on. Each block size depends on the relative value; the following is an example of how a block is described in the ECharts treemap API:

```
{
    "value": "1024.00",
    "name": "stackoverflow",
    "path": "stackoverflow",
    "children": [
```

```
{
  "value": 1,
  "name": "primary",
  "path": "stackoverflow/primary",
  "children": [
  {
    "value": "1024.00",
    "name": "0",
    "path": "stackoverflow/primary/0",
    "children": [
    {
      "value": 15,
      "name": "_d",
      "path": "stackoverflow/primary/0/_d"
```

In the preceding code, we can see that each element contains a `name`, a `path`, a `value` and a `children` element. `Name` and `value` speak for themselves, the `path` is the path in the treemap, and the children will be the blocks shown when you click and drill down.

This is a perfect match with what we are trying to achieve: we want to have the indices as the first level and see their size, then we want to drill down and display the shards with relative size, and then drill down and see segments and size.

But why not just create a new visualization for the Kibana dashboard? Well, the topology plugin will leverage the _cat API provided by Elasticsearch, a super powerful endpoint to access the essential stats of the cluster:
`https://www.elastic.co/guide/en/elasticsearch/reference/current/cat.html`

For this book, I've limited the scope of implementation to the index topology rendering, but there are a lot of opportunities to extend this plugin in the _cat API, which I will leave to your imagination.

As mentioned previously, the idea here is not to see how the plugin has been implemented line by line, but rather point you to what is important in order to make the plugin work in Kibana, either in the public code or in the server code. I've put the code base in the following GitHub repository:
`https://github.com/bahaaldine/packt-kibana-5.0/tree/master/chapter9/topology`.

Walking through topology implementation

In this part, we'll analyze the different parts of the code implementation, from the server-side code to the front side code.

Server code

We will start with the server-side code that will host the API needed to build a cluster topology. To do this, let's first examine a couple of files. The `index.js` file located at the root of the plugin is responsible for bootstrapping and loading the plugin when Kibana starts. To load the plugin, use this link: https://github.com/bahaaldine/packt-kibana-5.0/blob/master/chapter9/topology/index.js#L1.

This contains the following line:

```
import topologyRoutes from './server/routes/api';
```

The preceding line points to a file which contains all the service APIs the frontend-side can call. See here: https://github.com/bahaaldine/packt-kibana-5.0/blob/master/chapter9/topology/server/routes/api.js.

When you open the file, you will see the following list of available APIs:

```
import cat_indices from './cat_indices'
import cat_shards from './cat_shards'
import cat_segments from './cat_segments'
import get_cluster_topology from './get_cluster_topology'
export default function (server) {
  server = cat_indices(server);
  server = cat_shards(server);
  server = cat_segments(server);
  server = get_cluster_topology(server);
};
```

Each line in the exported function loads a different API in the `server` variable, which is essentially the Kibana server. Let us take a look at one of these files: https://github.com/bahaaldine/packt-kibana-5.0/blob/master/chapter9/topology/server/routes/cat_indices.js.

Here is what the `cat_indices.js` file contains:

```
import { catIndices } from './helpers';
import Promise from 'bluebird';
export default function (server) {
server.route({
  path: '/topology/indices',
  method: 'GET',
  handler: function (req, reply) {
      Promise.try(catIndices(server, req))
      .then(function(indices) {
```

```
      reply({indices: indices});
    });
  }
});

return server;
}
```

The preceding function describes an API that can be accessed in the `/topology/indices`
endpoint. It uses a `catIndices` helper function, found at
`https://github.com/bahaaldine/packt-kibana-5.0/blob/master/chapter9/topology/se
rver/routes/helpers.js#L3`, the implementation of which uses the Elasticsearch cat API,
as the following code snippet shows:

```
function catIndices(server) {
const client = server.plugins.elasticsearch.client;
return function() {
  return client.cat.indices({format: 'json'});
}
}
```

As a result of the preceding code, you will see that an Elasticsearch client is available as part
of the Kibana server API and can be used in the plugin for all operations that don't exceed
the scope of permissions that the internal Kibana server role has. You can't, for example,
create an index or template with this client. If you need to do that, you will need to
instantiate a new client, as shown in the following example:

```
new elasticsearch.Client(
  { host, ssl, plugins, keepAlive, defer, log}
);
```

If you try to include the preceding `catIndices` server-side API in your newly created
plugin, and call the ending at `https://localhost:5601/ujl/topology/indices`, you
should get the following type of output:

```
{
  "indices": [
    ...
    {
      "health": "green",
      "status": "open",
      "index": "stackoverflow",
      "uuid": "GPR8PhlwQwO9CLzf0pBSkA",
      "pri": "1",
      "rep": "0",
      "docs.count": "11192635",
      "docs.deleted": "0",
```

```
      "store.size": "1.8gb",
      "pri.store.size": "1.8gb"
    }
    ...
  ]
}
```

The preceding API will output a **JSON** formatted _cat API response. If you have included this API in your plugin, it's now available for the front side. Please note that, because we have launched Kibana in development mode, it adds a random string to the URL, so in this case you should have something different than /ujl/ in the path.

The following strategies are used to build the cluster topology object:

- We do it on the client side. In other words, we successively call the _cat/indices, _cat/shards, and _cat/segments APIs, and we build the expected document there, pass it to ECharts, and render the treemap.
- We build the document on the server side by combining the API calls, mapping the data, and returning a proper treemap document to the frontend.

I think that delegating this responsibility to the server side is a better approach, since we want to lower the implementation complexity on the frontend. We will also be able to reuse this API, if needed.

As the catIndices API, the getClusterTopology API has its own file (https://github.com/bahaaldine/packt-kibana-5.0/blob/master/chapter9/topology/server/routes/get_cluster_topology.js) and uses the getClusterTopology helper to build the cluster index topology: https://github.com/bahaaldine/packt-kibana-5.0/blob/master/chapter9/topology/server/routes/helpers.js#L66.

Let's peel out this function.

First it uses the _cat/indices API to fetch all the indices:

```
    return client.cat.indices({format:
    'json'}).then(function(catIndicesResponse) {
      catIndicesResponse.map(index => {
        topology.indices[index.index] = { ...index };
        topology.indices[index.index].shards = { p:{} , r:{} };
      });
```

Then it builds a comma-separated string that contains all the indices' names, to query the subsequent _cat/shard and _cat/segment APIs:

```
const indexNames = catIndicesResponse.map(index => {
return index.index;
}).join(',');
```

It then adds the shard API response to the main topology variable:

```
return client.cat.shards({format: 'json', index:
indexNames}).then(function(catShardsResponse) {
catShardsResponse.map(shard => {
topology.indices[shard.index].shards[shard.prirep][shard.shard] = {
...shard };
topology.indices[shard.index].shards[shard.prirep][shard.shard].segments =
{};
});
```

The same goes for the segments:

```
return client.cat.segments({format: 'json', index:
indexNames}).then(function(catSegmentsResponse) {
catSegmentsResponse.map(segment => {

if ( typeof
topology.indices[segment.index].shards[segment.prirep][segment.shard] !=
"undefined" ) {
topology.indices[segment.index].shards[segment.prirep][segment.shard].segme
nts[segment.segment] = { ...segment };
}
});
```

The way the shards are added to their relative indices, and the segments to their relative shards, is just by using the index name, shard name, and segment name returned by the _cat/shards and _cat/segements:

```
{
"shards": [
...
{
"index": "stackoverflow",
"shard": "0",
"prirep": "p",
"state": "STARTED",
"docs": "11192635",
"store": "1.8gb",
"ip": "127.0.0.1",
"node": "Ju_HqBW"
```

```
}
...
    ]
}
{
"segments": [
...
{
"index": "stackoverflow",
"shard": "0",
"prirep": "p",
"ip": "127.0.0.1",
"segment": "_d",
"generation": "13",
"docs.count": "73700",
"docs.deleted": "0",
"size": "15.1mb",
"size.memory": "94765",
"committed": "true",
"searchable": "true",
"version": "6.2.0",
"compound": "false"
}
...
]
}
```

Then, for example, to affect a shard to an index, the following path is built based on the API response values:

```
topology.indices[shard.index].shards[shard.prirep][shard.shard] = {
...shard };
```

At this point, we have built a topology document that looks as follows:

```
{
  "indices": {
    "stackoverflow": {
      "health": "green",
      "status": "open",
      "index": "stackoverflow",
      "uuid": "GPR8PhlwQwO9CLzf0pBSkA",
      "pri": "1",
      "rep": "0",
      "docs.count": "11192635",
      "docs.deleted": "0",
      "store.size": "1.8gb",
      "pri.store.size": "1.8gb",
```

```
"shards": {
  "p": {
  "0": {
  "index": "stackoverflow",
  "shard": "0",
  "prirep": "p",
  "state": "STARTED",
  "docs": "11192635",
  "store": "1.8gb",
  "ip": "127.0.0.1",
  "node": "Ju_HqBW",
  "segments": {
    "_d": {
    "index": "stackoverflow",
    "shard": "0",
    "prirep": "p",
    "ip": "127.0.0.1",
    "segment": "_d",
    "generation": "13",
    "docs.count": "73700",
    "docs.deleted": "0",
    "size": "15.1mb",
    "size.memory": "94765",
    "committed": "true",
    "searchable": "true",
    "version": "6.2.0",
    "compound": "false"
```

However, this is not exactly what we want. That's where buildChartData
(https://github.com/bahaaldine/packt-kibana-5.0/blob/master/chapter9/topology/s
erver/routes/helpers.js#L34) comes into play.

This applies a succession of mapping functions to the topology document to create the
expected treemap document shown earlier.

I'll just take the example of the segment children object building to illustrate the process:

```
children: _.map(shardItem.segments, (segmentItem, segmentName) => {
  return {
    value: toMB(segmentItem['size']),
    name: segmentName,
    path: indexName + "/" + shardTypeName + "/" + shardName + "/" +
segmentName
  }
})
```

Each parent leaf (indices and shards) gets a `children` nested document in which the children are populated. Each leaf (parent or children) has a value in megabytes, a name, corresponding in the preceding example to the segment name, and the path built out of the index name, the shard name, and the segment name.

At this point, we have built our treemap document; we now just need to call the API from the frontend public code.

Public code

Our application only has one page, the landing page, whose files are located here:

`https://github.com/bahaaldine/packt-kibana-5.0/tree/master/chapter9/topology/public/views`.

There are three files:

- `index.html`: The actual HTML template
- `index.js`: The JavaScript file that contains the Angular code (controller and directive)
- `index.less`: The file containing our stylesheet

As mentioned previously, Angular is the framework used by Kibana, so I've tried to limit the number of Angular features I'm using here. I've actually just used the notion of the Angular directive (`https://docs.angularjs.org/guide/directive`), which essentially allows us to create reusable components. We'll come to that shortly.

There is another file which is very important, too: the `topology` class (`https://github.com/bahaaldine/packt-kibana-5.0/blob/master/chapter9/topology/public/common/Topology.js`), which is the object that will provide the server-side API to the frontend:

```
class Topology {
constructor() {
  }
getClusterTopology() {
return $http.get(chrome.addBasePath('/topology/cluster'));
  }
}
```

The implementation is pretty basic, and only exposes a default `constructor` method and a `getClusterTopology` method that calls our server-side `/topology/cluster` endpoint.

Now, if you take a look at the `index.html` file (https://github.com/bahaaldine/packt-kibana-5.0/blob/master/chapter9/topology/public/views/index.html), you will see that it's pretty basic and contains a minimal amount of HTML code. The important portion is the following HTML tag:

```
<div cluster-topology flex style="width: 100%; min-height: 250px; height:
650px" flex class="cluster-topology"></div>
```

This contains the attribute `cluster-topology` that triggers the `clusterTopology` execution in the `index.js` file at https://github.com/bahaaldine/packt-kibana-5.0/blob/master/chapter9/topology/public/views/index.js.

The directive instantiates a `topology` object and calls the server-side API, then passes the response to build the treemap series data:

```
$scope.topology = new Topology();
$scope.topology.getClusterTopology().then( response => {
...
series: [{
name: 'Topology',
type: 'treemap',
data: response.data,
leafDepth: 1,
levels: [ ...]
...
```

Plugin installation

In the previous sections, we have seen how to run a plugin in development mode with the help of both:

- `gulp sync`: This command synchronizes the plugin in the Kibana installation directory
- `gulp dev`: This command synchronizes all the changes we made during the plugin development

So in development, whenever you hit the save button, refresh the browser, you should see the latest version of your plugin.

In production, things are slightly different, plugins need to be built and deploy either manually or using your preferred continuous integration tools.

In this section, we'll go through the all the minimal steps to build and install the plugin. You will first need to access via a terminal the plugin directory and run the following command:

```
gulp package
```

This command will first remove a build directory, if a build directory exists. The build directory contains plugin builds.

Then it will compile all the code and finally package it as a kibana plugin build, in the target directory.

After running the command, you should have a new topology build in the target directory suffixed by the plugin version, for example `topology-5.0.0.tar.gz`.

Now we need to install the plugin in our production Kibana instance. The basic step to do it is to run the following command in the Kibana installation directory:

```
bin/kibana-plugin install file:///path/to/the/plugin/build
```

In this command, you need to replace the last argument by the path to the plugin build.

If you try to install the plugin and run a Kibana instance, you should get the following results:

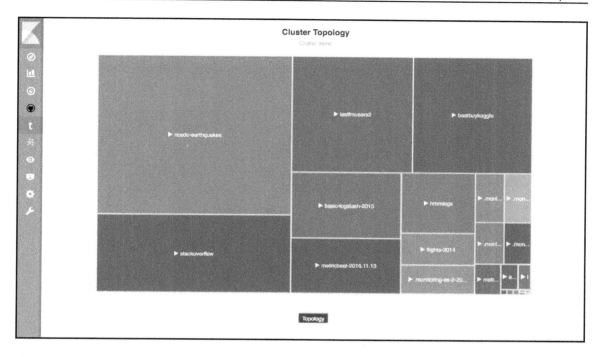

If you try to hand over the **stackoverflow** index, you should get the size of the index:

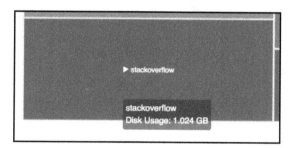

Then, if you drill down to the segment, you will see all the segments and their sizes on the disk:

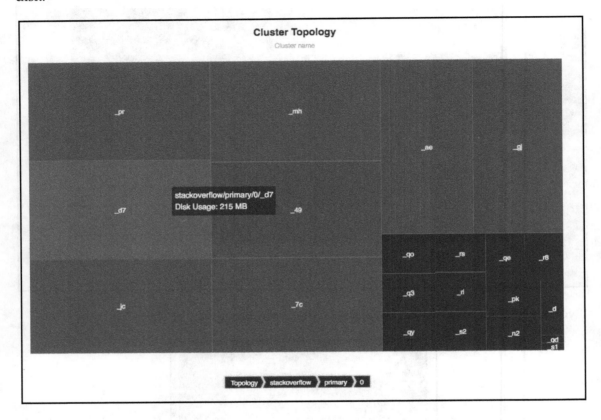

Summary

At this point, we are pretty much done with custom plugin implementation in Kibana.

We have been through the generation of a bare Kibana plugin, and how the plugin is structured and how the environment should be prepared with regards to custom plugin implementation requirements. We have also seen how the service-side code and the front side code works together and how to build and install the plugin in a target environment.

Finally, I hope that this topology will help you to get a better idea of the distribution of the data across all the indices.

This concludes, I hope, an interesting ride through all the new and exciting Kibana 5.0 features. I hope you have enjoyed the reading and now have a good understanding of how Kibana 5.0 can serve a very large variety of use cases.

Index

www.ingramcontent.com/pod-product-compliance
Lightning Source LLC
Chambersburg PA
CBHW060525060326
40690CB00017B/3382